# SURFING
## A Beginner's Guide

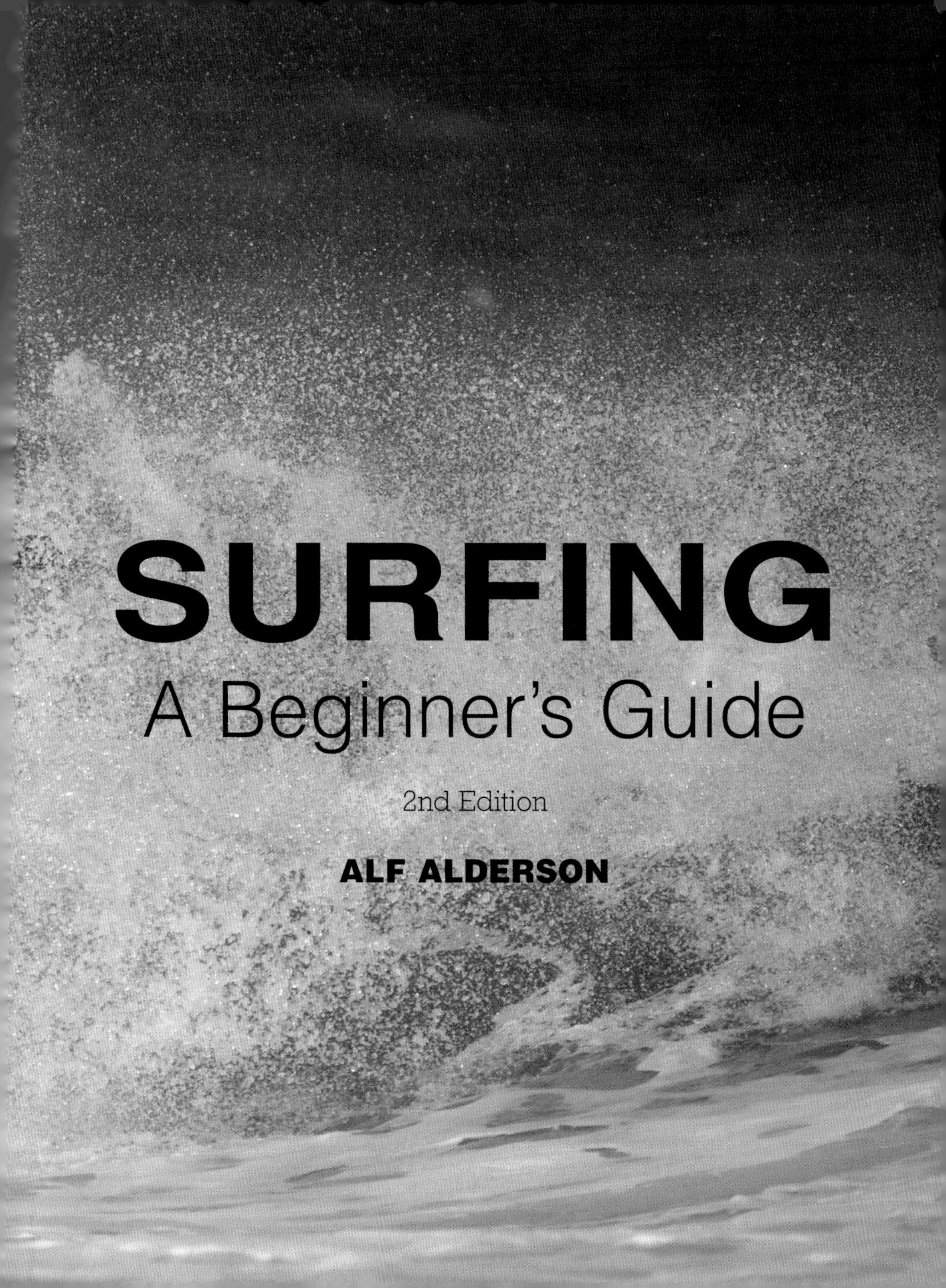

# SURFING

## A Beginner's Guide

2nd Edition

**ALF ALDERSON**

Copyright © 2008 John Wiley & Sons Ltd, The Atrium, Southern Gate, Chichester,

West Sussex PO19 8SQ, England

Telephone (+44) 1243 779777

Email (for orders and customer service enquiries): cs-books@wiley.co.uk

Visit our Home Page on www.wiley.com

Photography © 2008 Sean Davey

Other Wiley Editorial Offices

John Wiley & Sons Inc., 111 River Street, Hoboken, NJ 07030, USA

Jossey-Bass, 989 Market Street, San Francisco, CA 94103-1741, USA

Wiley-VCH Verlag GmbH, Boschstr. 12, D-69469 Weinheim, Germany

John Wiley & Sons Australia Ltd, 42 McDougall Street, Milton, Queensland 4064, Australia

John Wiley & Sons (Asia) Pte Ltd, 2 Clementi Loop #02-01, Jin Xing Distripark, Singapore 129809

John Wiley & Sons Canada Ltd, 6045 Freemont Blvd. Mississauga, Ontario, L5R 4J3 Canada

Wiley also publishes its books in a variety of electronic formats. Some content that appears in print may not be available in electronic books.

Library of Congress Cataloging-in-Publication Data

Alderson, Wayne Alf.

Surfing: a beginner's guide/Wayne Alf Alderson. -- 2nd ed. p. cm.

Originally published: Arundel, West Sussex: Fernhurst Books, 1996.

ISBN 978-0-470-51654-6 (pbk.: alk. paper)

1. Surfing--Handbooks, manuals, etc. I. Title.

GV840.S8A395 2008

797.3'2--dc22

2007050387

British Library Cataloguing in Publication Data

A catalogue record for this book is available from the British Library

ISBN: 978-0-470-51654-6 (PB)

Typeset in the UK by Artmedia Press, London

Printed and bound in Italy by Printer Trento, Trento

This book is printed on acid-free paper responsibly manufactured from sustainable forestry in which at least two trees are planted for each one used for paper production.

# CONTENTS

# PREFACE

Since the early 1980s the popularity of surfing has grown almost exponentially, and thanks to improvements in wetsuit technology there are few coastlines in the world that haven't been surfed now – even Alaska and Norway have resident surfers these days.

Despite this, surfing is still one of the hardest sports to learn and master. So in this book you'll find all the basics you need to get you going – what you won't find is the lowdown on how to pull aerials or ride 15-foot reef breaks – by the time you're ready for that, you won't be needing an instruction book.

One of the world's top young pro surfers, Flynn Novak, is captured in action by world-class surf photographer Sean Davey in step-by-step sequences that beautifully illustrate just what it should look like when you get to your feet for the first time or pull off your first cutback. And hopefully the words alongside should help to bring it all together in one neat and easily assimilated package!

If the surf conditions are right, you're reasonably fit, a competent swimmer and determined enough, you should be able to reach a basic level of surfing within two to three days. You may not be ripping the waves apart, but you will be standing up on the board with a modicum of control. Then it's a case of practice, practice, practice and lots of commitment. I've known people who changed their entire lifestyle to improve their surfing, but once you've got the basics wired you can still have a great time in the surf even if you never get beyond being a 'weekend warrior'.

Whatever your aspirations, there are few sports that get you hooked the way surfing does. It doesn't matter whether you become a contest hotshot or a mellow soul who wants to cruise along on gentle beach breaks – once you're riding waves you're guaranteed to be having as much fun (almost ...) as anyone can without their clothes on.

Alf Alderson
St. David's, Pembrokeshire, Spring 2008

# Equipment

'There's no sport that I know of that has all the ingredients of pure enjoyment that surfing does.'
Peter Cole, legendary big wave rider

The majority of surfers are still riding shortboards, despite the resurgence of longboards, mini-mals, funboards, and a wide range of 'hybrid' designs in recent years.

Choosing the right board is essential if you want to make good progress as a beginner, but it's not just a case of walking into your friendly local surf shop and sauntering out again 15 minutes later ready to rip.

Surfboard design is an art form in itself, and no two surfers will ride the same board in the same way or get the same out of it. This is not the place to go into detail on the intricacies of board design (see Chapter 7), but we can take a look at the most popular board designs out there.

## SHORTBOARDS

The majority of shortboards will be three-fin 'thrusters', usually within the size range 5 ft 8 in/1.70 m to 6 ft 8 in/2.0 m. Bigger surfers may go for slightly longer boards; longer shortboards (excuse the oxymoron) are used in bigger surf; and some surfers will opt for shorter, high performance models.

Shortboards are basically for more experienced surfers, being highly manoeuvrable, but at the same time more difficult to control. Various features of the board will be designed to suit a surfer's riding style. Thickness and width vary from board to board, as do rocker and vee. Rails may be hard or soft, the board may have channels, the fin configuration can differ, and tail shape will also vary. (If all this is as clear as mud, see Chapter 7 to understand the terminology.) As you can see there's a lot more to a surfboard than meets the eye, and a lot of time and money is spent on board design and development.

You should forget about getting a high performance shortboard if you're just starting out – it may look cool on the beach, but it will do you no favours in the surf. You'll find it difficult to paddle, difficult to catch waves with, and difficult to ride. What you should be looking for is a funboard or a mini-mal.

A modern epoxy shortboard.

A modern custom-made fiberglass shortboard.

# FUNBOARDS

Funboards sit mid-way between a shortboard and a longboard. They'll usually be around 7 ft 6 in/2.30 m in length, and be wider and thicker than a shortboard, with a more rounded nose. These boards are basically designed for having fun on, as the name implies. They make it easy to catch waves, but are still manoeuvrable enough to allow you to challenge yourself in the surf, and they're a great option if you surf in an area where the waves are generally small or lacking in power. They're especially good for beginners but are often used by experienced older surfers looking for an advantage in catching the waves.

**A custom-made fibreglass funboard.**

# LONGBOARDS AND MINI-MALS

Longboards are the boards that are associated with the halcyon days of the '60s, when they were known as Malibu boards after the famous California point break. Everyone who was anyone 'rode the nose' at every opportunity and drop-knee turns were the only turns worth doing. They were superseded in the late '60s and early '70s by shortboards, but made a come-back in the late '80s, and now most breaks will have a number of longboards out in the line-up.

A 'longboard' is generally considered to be over 9 ft/3 m in length with a much more rounded nose than the previous two categories, and a wider and thicker template. They may have one or more fins.

Mini-mals are kind of 'short' longboards of between 7 ft 6 in/2.30 m and 8 ft 6 in/2.60 m in length, and they're another good option for learning on as they offer a lot of flotation and stability and are easier to paddle. However, in big surf they can be bulky for beginners to handle.

**A modern epoxy longboard.**

Longboards are the least manoeuvrable of the three main categories of surfboard and are ridden in a different way. The style is generally much smoother and more graceful than that of the shortboarder, with an emphasis on 'walking the board' (moving up and down on the deck of the board) and nose riding (surfing with five or ten toes over the nose – 'hang five' and 'hang ten' respectively). Having said that, high performance longboard surfing, featuring shortboard-style moves is becoming increasingly common as well as easier on modern, lighter, performance-oriented models.

# POP-OUTS

A pop-out can be any of the above designs produced from a mould, whereas a custom board is shaped and finished by hand. A pop-out makes an excellent first board for a number of reasons. For a start a new pop-out will be about a third of the price of a new custom board, as well as being much sturdier and far less prone to damage. Pop-outs don't have the same smooth flowing lines as custom boards, being thicker and wider and somewhat more rough and ready due to the moulding process, but at this stage you don't need the design refinements that custom boards provide.

**Cheap n' cheerful – a 'pop out', great for beginners.**

# SOFT BOARDS

Probably the ideal boards for beginners. Generally around 7 ft 6 in/2.30 m long, soft boards are buoyant and stable, and since they're made of relatively soft polyurethane foam they don't hurt as much if they hit you on a wipeout. This can be a real confidence booster for first-timers who are already being knocked all over by the waves without having the additional worry of being hit by a big lump of fibreglass.

**Easy to learn on (it's even got handles!) and safe to use – a soft top board.**

# BODY BOARDS

Body boarding/boogie boarding is the easy option for anyone who has neither the time, the skill nor the patience to learn stand-up surfing. But it's not real surfing, so that's the last you'll be hearing of it in this book.

# CHOOSING YOUR BOARD

Get a board that will help you to improve rather than one that simply looks good. A soft board or pop-out is the best option but if you really want to go for a custom board, a funboard or a mini-mal style is best. What you're looking for at this stage is flotation and stability in the board, which will make the difficult task of balancing on it that much easier. Ideally you should look for something between 12 in/30 cm and 18 in/45 cm longer than you are tall. Most boards these days have three fins, although for a beginner a single-fin board is perfectly adequate (and is also two less fins to potentially get bashed by when you wipe out).

You'll find that prices vary from area to area, so shop around. A good surf shop should be able to advise you on what sort of board is most appropriate for your skills. It's best if you can also take along a friend who already surfs to provide some advice. Unless you have plenty of cash, it's also well worth considering a second-hand board as at this stage you don't actually know if you're going to like surfing (although if you don't you should seek medical advice as it's quite possible you're dead). A good second-hand board can be picked up for around half the price of a new one, and some surf shops may even let you give it a trial run which is never the case with a new board.

Be careful with second-hand boards though. They've all had their fair share of knocks, and if the foam is starting to discolour in too many places (where it's let in water through a damaged surface) it's usually best to leave it. Also check for soft spots on the deck where the fibreglass may be delaminating from the foam. And if the board doesn't have changeable fins, ensure there are no cracks around the base of the fins where they join the board.

**A shortie – ideal for warm summer conditions when there's no more than a slight chill.**

# WETSUITS

A wetsuit keeps you warm by trapping a thin layer of water close to your body, which is then warmed by your body heat. This is often flushed out when you wipeout so the suit needs to be a tight fit.

The kind of wetsuit you need will obviously depend where you surf, and can vary, for example, from something like a 5/4/3 mm full steamer for cold climates (a combination of 5 mm, 4 mm, and 3 mm thick neoprene on different areas of the 'wettie'), to nothing more than a 2-mm vest or spring suit for warm areas. Developments in wetsuit and neoprene technology in recent years have resulted in design standards, warmth and comfort that were unthinkable when the first edition of this book was written, and with a good wetsuit you should never feel the cold too badly in all but the most miserable climates.

**Short-sleeved full suit – a good option for summer in temperate waters.**

**Full suit – for cooler/cold waters, depending on thickness.**

Fit is everything with a wetsuit. Get advice from a surf shop and/or surfie friends, but trying a suit on and stretching and bending in it is the only way to be sure it's going to fit properly and be comfortable.

Your wetsuit shouldn't be too tight, but should fit snugly everywhere on your body with the possible exception of your shoulders where you need a bit of room for paddling. If there are any folds of neoprene it's too big; if you are having trouble breathing and the blood supply to your wrists and ankles is feeling restricted, it's obviously too small.

Full wetsuits come in a wide variety of styles, particularly with regard to the zip (which in most cases goes at the back!). Some zips are longer than others, which makes it easier to get the suit on and off but also easier for water to get in, whilst zipperless suits provide the best protection of all but can be a bugger to get on and off and are also prone to tearing around the 'entrance' point unless you treat them carefully.

You'll also find different manufacturing techniques (cross stitch, blind stitch, double blind stitch, 'liquid' glue seams, taped seams, etc. – the warmest is a combination of blind stitch and glued and taped seams), different types of neoprene, and different thicknesses of neoprene. The best way around this confusion is to ask the advice of friends or the surf shop staff in the area where you intend to surf, as they'll know what's most appropriate for the local surf.

Many experienced surfers have different wetsuits for winter and summer, and maybe one for spring and autumn as well. As a beginner you don't really want to fork out on a whole wardrobe of neoprene, so go for whatever will allow you to get in the water most often in the most comfort.

You can readily find second-hand wetsuits, but look carefully for holes, rips, tears and patches. Once a wetsuit starts to fall apart there's only so much you can do to stop it, and most repair jobs do little more than delay the inevitable. They can also make the suit more uncomfortable to wear.

## SURF TIPS

- Go for function not fashion with your first board – you'll be riding waves sooner.
- Don't be afraid to ask for advice from surfie friends and in surf shops.
- Make sure your wetsuit is a good fit – even if it costs. Otherwise you won't enjoy yourself in the surf and learning will be slower.
- Watch out for the sun – even in cold climates you can burn.
- Protect your inner ears with some sort of ear plugs, especially if you surf in cool waters. This will avoid you developing 'surfer's ear'.
- After you've used your wetsuit, always rinse it in fresh water. This will extend its life and also stop it from smelling!

# RASH VESTS

A rash vest is an invaluable and relatively cheap accessory – a close fitting Lycra vest worn under a wetsuit, which stops the wetsuit seams from rubbing. In the days before they were 'invented', several consecutive days of surfing would often lead to a surfer having horrendous wetsuit rubs around the shoulders and armpits, especially with a poorly fitting suit. Rash vests are also useful as protection from the sun when surfing in board shorts.

**Keeps the sun off, stops wax rash – a rash vest (doesn't cause rashes despite the name!).**

## ADDITIONAL NEOPRENE

Depending on where you surf and your tolerance to cold you may also need to buy neoprene boots, gloves or mitts, and a hood. In cold climates these can be a necessity rather than a luxury. Boots are also useful to avoid spiked feet on reefs and in waters where sea urchins lurk. These should be a good fit or they end up like water-filled balloons around your feet.

## EXTRAS

### LEASHES

The leash attaches to your ankle (above whichever foot is to the rear of the board), and basically stops you from losing the board after a wipeout. They're made of stretchy urethane, with a Velcro ankle strap, and attach to the 'deck plug' on the board. Make sure you have a bomb-proof knot, and that the leash doesn't pass across the rail (edge) of the board when at full stretch, otherwise it can cut through the board, especially if it's a fibreglass model. Most leashes come with a 'railsaver' to prevent this.

While leashes are obviously of great value, preventing long unwanted swims and loose boards from hurtling towards shore, they should be used properly. Make sure the leash is the recommended length for your board and the size of waves you'll be riding, and after a wipeout cover your head/face with your hands on surfacing. The leash can occasionally bring the board skimming back across the water towards you, and the first thing that surfaces will be the first thing it hits – your head.

Leashes can also tangle around things such as rocks, your feet and small dogs, so always take up the slack when carrying your board. Most people wrap their leash around the fins and tail.

## NOSE GUARDS

This is a rubber guard for the nose of a short board, one of the most accident-prone areas. It will also prevent you from being speared by the board in a wipeout. An over-priced but useful accessory.

# WAX/DECK GRIP

One undervalued aspect of wax is that it supplies the classic introduction for lone surfers at a strange break – 'Got any wax, mate?' It's simple stuff, easily forgotten, but you can't surf without it on the deck of your board. Made from a mixture of paraffin and beeswax, surf wax comes in different hardnesses for different water temperatures. Most waxes have some sort of exotic smell such as coconut to evoke memories of warmer waters for those of us far removed from swaying palms, and they also come in a variety of colours, with brand names relying heavily on rubbish sexual double entendres.

A useful accessory if you use wax is wax comb. This allows you to roughen up the surface of old wax on your board, which can tend to lose its 'grippiness' after a while. However, you will eventually need to remove the wax and put on a fresh coat.

If you surf without a wetsuit you'll find the wax can rub and cause a rash on your chest, stomach and the inside of your legs. A combination of rash vest and long boardshorts will prevent this.

As an alternative to wax you can use deck grip, a rubber patch that sticks to the board and gives a good grippy surface for your feet. It also provides some protection against delamination of the deck resulting from the weight of the rider. Make sure your deck is totally clean before application otherwise it won't stick. It's ridiculously expensive but unlike wax it only needs applying once.

**Deck grip – keeps your feet on the board (in theory).**

The largest wave in the world occurs every day on every beach in the form of the tide. It has a wave-length of half the circumference of the Earth, travels at 700–800 miles an hour, and 'breaks' once every 12 hours and 25 minutes.

## SUN PROTECTION

In the surf you're very prone to sunburn, not only from direct sunlight but also from reflection from the water. Wear a high factor waterproof sun cream or even total blockout, especially if you have fair skin, and re-apply frequently. This is especially important in warmer climates, but even in colder areas you can easily suffer sunburn if you're in the water for a long time in summer. In addition, rash vests are a good way of protecting your upper body from the sun without getting too hot.

## EAR PROTECTION

Anyone who surfs on a regular basis, especially in cold water, should seriously consider wearing ear plugs in the water. The reason? Cold water and cold winds can, over a long period of time, cause a bony growth in the ear canal. This is the body's attempt to protect the inner ear from cold, and eventually it can lead to water becoming trapped in the ear and even partial deafness. It can be treated, but this involves painful surgery and the growth can recur. Most surf shops in cold climates should stock ear plugs. Blu-Tack is a cheap but effective alternative.

## BOARD PROTECTION

Custom surfboards in particular are fragile and expensive, so it's worthwhile investing in a board bag to protect your investment. There is a huge range available for all sizes of board, and some will take two or more.

## HEAD PROTECTION

Personally I like to keep the gear I wear in the water to a minimum, but I can see that helmets have their uses in big, gnarly waves. You don't see helmets used that often and they're rather cumbersome but if you're worried about bashing your noggin on rocks, board or fins, check one out.

# First Steps

'Surfing expresses ... a pure yearning for visceral,
physical contact with the natural world.'
Matt Warshaw, Maverick's: The Story of Big-Wave Surfing

# GETTING FIT

## 'Surfing is for life.'
Bruce Jenkins, North Shore Chronicles

You've got your equipment, now to use it. But hold on, not so fast – there are a few things you can do before hitting the surf that will make the learning experience more rewarding and effective.

The first is to get as fit as you can. Surfing requires strength, speed, stamina and agility, and anything you can do to improve these will be well worthwhile. You should think specifically about developing your arms, shoulders, are upper back and neck, and improving your cardiovascular fitness and overall agility. Of course the best form of exercise and the most enjoyable is surfing itself, but getting in trim before you start and then keeping surf fit will pay dividends.

## SWIMMING

You should be able to swim AT LEAST 50 METRES IN OPEN WATER to ensure your own safety if you get into difficulty. Swimming, whether in the local pool, or better still the sea (maybe in your new wetsuit – a good way to get a feel for it) is the perfect exercise for surfing – not only does it improve/maintain your fitness, but many of the muscles you use are the same as those used in surfing, especially if you do the crawl.

## HOME EXERCISES

There isn't the space here to go into specific exercise routines, but any library or the Internet will have books that can help, or you could join a gym and get a tailor-made training programme.

## BALANCE SPORTS

Associated 'balance' sports can also be useful and fun ways of toning up for surfing. Snowboarding and skateboarding are more or less snow and land-based versions of surfing, with similar manoeuvres and very similar balance techniques involved, and for cold-climate surfers snowboarding makes an excellent winter alternative.

Balance boards such as the Indo Board are also a really good – although pretty over-priced – way of practising your technique on dry land.

## SURF SCHOOLS

While this book aims to teach you the basics of surfing, you really can't beat direct tuition on the beach or out in the surf. Try to get some lessons from a qualified surfing instructor, as it undoubtedly speeds up the learning process and makes you more safety conscious. There are surf schools on most coastlines that are popular with surfers. You can get contact details from the relevant surfing association (see Chapter 10 for details) or just go to the Internet.

**Back to school – Gabe Davies of Surf Solutions Surf School in Hossegor imparting knowledge on the beach.**

# *SHORE SURFING*

If you have access to a swimming pool in which you can take your board, or more practically, the sea in flat conditions, why not get in some paddling practice? OK, it doesn't look too cool, but this is one of the most strenuous aspects of learning to surf, and the more you can practice it the better. For more details on paddling technique see the next chapter.

Another useful exercise on dry land is getting to your feet on your board. But make sure you do it on a soft surface, and remove the fins, otherwise you could easily damage your board. This is only really recommended for soft skin and pop-out boards – custom fibreglass boards will damage too easily.

To do this, first of all lie on your board. Assuming that you have a good beginner's board of around 7 ft 6 in/2.30 m in length, you should have your feet about 6 inches/15 cms from the back of the board when you're lying on it. This will obviously depend on how tall you are, but basically there should be about 10–12 inches/30 cm of the nose of the board lifted off the water surface when you are paddling it if your weight is distributed evenly on the deck. As the board is not on the water you can't really judge that, but you can usually sense what feels right.

Put both hands flat on the deck directly under your shoulders and push up as if you were actually doing a push-up. Take your body weight on your arms and hands. Once your upper body is off the board, bring your forward leg up under your chin, at the same time twisting your hips so your backside faces out to one side.

Your rear foot should follow so that you're now in a crouching position with your feet about shoulder width apart down the centreline of the board. Quickly stand up straight, with both feet flat on the board and still the same width apart, and your arms out to your sides for balance. Both feet should have the stringer running under the middle of them, and be at approximately 90 degrees to the stringer along the centreline of the board.

This whole movement should take less than a second to perform in one fluid motion. Don't worry if it's a bit stilted at first, as it will come in time. Watch experienced surfers taking off on a wave and you hardly even notice them get to their feet – they seem to be suddenly standing and riding.

Try to avoid introducing a 'halfway' stage of kneeling on the board before getting to your feet. Once you're on a wave this will make getting to your feet both slower and more difficult, and it's a very bad habit to get into – you'll never see an experienced surfer do this.

Practising like this is of course no substitute for the real thing, so now let's hit the beach.

'Paddling for the wave'. Note the position on the board – not too far forward, not too far back.

**Slide the hands back, ready to push up on the board.**

**Try to get to your feet in one fluid movement.**

**Fully standing, legs flexed.**

# ON THE BEACH

## CARRYING YOUR STICK

Before getting to the basics of wave riding, there are a few simple points worth considering. First, carrying the board. Now this may seem the kind of thing any fool can do, but some fools get it wrong. Don't, for example, drag your board behind you – it won't do the board any good, and just looks slack. Also, don't let the leash drag behind you. Once again it's bad for the equipment, and you or someone else may trip over it.

## WAXING-UP

To read some surf magazine features you could be forgiven for thinking there's an art to applying wax. All that's involved is common sense. You may want to apply a base coat which helps the top coat adhere, but with either coat give the board a good covering. Rub the block over the board lengthwise then crosswise or in a circular motion, until you get small bumps of wax appearing on the deck.

**Flynn applies fresh wax to an already waxed board.**

Apply a fresh layer every time you surf until it starts to get too lumpy and dirty (it should be fairly obvious when this stage is reached), at which point it can be scraped off with a hard, smooth edge (such as a credit card) after being left to melt in the sun.

Make sure you get the right wax for the water you're surfing in. Warm-water wax will be difficult to apply in cold conditions, and in warm weather cold-water wax will just smear across the deck and refuse to stick. In hot climates it's a good idea to cool the deck of your board in the sea before waxing up as it will help the wax go on more easily. Finally, don't rest your board on a hard or uneven surface when you wax it – the pressure you apply could ding the underside.

# INTO THE SURF

Those cool green cylinders peeling into the beach may look inviting, especially as you see another surfer cruising along one, but there's a lot of hard work involved in getting out to them.

First of all, check the waves. Sit on the beach for a few minutes watching the waves break. How big are they? Check the size against other surfers in the water. Is it crowded? More chance of collisions, especially for beginners. Are there any obvious rips and currents? These can be very dangerous if you don't know how to deal with them. Is the wave suitable for your level of ability? You want a gentle, rolling break rather than a heavy, pounding one. Make sure you're comfortable with all these factors before going out into the surf.

Once you get to the water's edge, attach your leash. Clean any sand and gunge out of the Velcro on the ankle strap, and ensure the cord itself is on the outside of your ankle. If it's on the inside there's more chance of getting snagged up on it. Now wade out in the water with your board nose-first under your arm, lifting it over approaching waves, until you're about knee-deep. At this point float the board beside you with the nose pointing out to sea, again lifting it over oncoming waves. Never place it in front of you – an oncoming wave can easily push it straight into your chest or face.

**Ensure you put your leash on properly – you don't want it coming off in the surf.**

Checking out the surf is always a good idea before you dash in, especially at an unfamiliar break.

Entering the water, board tucked comfortably under your arm.

Keep one or both hands on the deck to control the board as you're pushing it out. You can also rest your weight on the board if you're walking across an uneven or rocky sea bed to help you balance and/or to stop the rocks from cutting into your feet. If a wave catches you by surprise, try to hold onto your board. The easy option may be to let it go, safe in the knowledge that it's attached by the leash, but there may be someone behind you for it to bounce off. If you really have to let it go, check there is no-one behind you first. (See 'Safe Surfing' in Chapter 5.)

Research indicates that 10% of all waves are over 20 feet/6 metres in height, and 25% are between 3–4 feet/1.0–1.20 metres.

Approaching an oncoming wave – make sure the board is at your side to avoid its being pushed back into you and lift it over the wave as it passes, then continue to wade out with the board by your side.

# 'BELLYBOARDING'

Once you get into waist- to chest-deep water, turn the board shorewards when you get a lull in the surf. To start off with you're going to 'prone in' to the beach as if you were riding a bellyboard – this will give you a feel for the board and the surf.

To do this, wait until a broken wave approaches you, and when it's about two metres away push off the bottom with your feet and lie on your board, all the time holding a rail in each hand. Try to get into the position we discussed earlier – not too far forward or too far back. Too far forward and the board will 'pearl' which means the nose will dive under the water and you'll be thrown over the front; too far back and you'll have difficulty catching the wave.

As the wave picks you up, slide your weight back a little to avoid nose-diving, then once you're moving slide forward again. If you lean one way or the other you'll find the board will turn in the same direction – try this to get some idea how the board reacts to shifts in body weight.

After you've done this a few times, you should start paddling for the approaching wave rather than just hoping it will pick you up of its own accord. Lie on the board, looking over your shoulder at the approaching wave. Start to paddle for it when it's about four metres away, using alternate strokes. When you feel the wave pick you up, paddle one or two more strokes to ensure you've caught it, then lift your arms out of the water, grip the rails and ride into the beach. Adjust your weight back and forwards on the board as necessary to stop it nose-diving or stalling.

The wave has picked up the surfer, who grips the rails for balance and makes slight adjustments of body weight to allow the board to trim, retaining maximum planing speed. Note how he keeps his head well up so he can see what's coming.

## STOPPING THE BOARD

You may need to get off the board before the wave has faded away under you, especially if you're on a collision course with someone else! To do this, either slide off the side of the board holding firmly onto the rails, or move to the back causing the tail to dig in and stall the board.

## TRAVERSING THE WAVE

The next step is to bellyboard across the face of the wave rather than straight into the beach. Paddle for the wave as above, and once you've caught it lean left or right until the board turns. Don't be too brutal about this or you'll probably fall off. If you do it gently you should feel the board start to turn, and as long as you keep the weight lightly angled on that side of the board you will find yourself traversing along the wave. If you maintain too much weight on the rail the board may turn over the top of the wave. By shifting your weight around you may even be able to make the board do shallow 'S' turns along the wave as you ride towards shore.

Once you're catching waves easily and bellyboarding with confidence, you're ready to have a go at standing up.

# STANDING UP

So this is it, the hardest thing you'll come across in learning to surf. Once you've mastered this the rest will follow sooner or later if you stick at it.

Walk out with your board to the same point where you were bellyboarding and in a lull between sets turn the board shorewards, then lie on it. Keep checking behind you for the next set. Give about four hard strokes on each side, and when the approaching wave picks you up give a couple more. Then go through the motions you practised on the beach as quickly as possible: This all sounds like a hell of a lot to remember while you are struggling with an unfamiliar object in an unfamiliar medium, but understanding the technique

1. Paddle powerfully with both arms to match the speed of the wave, which then picks up the board.

2. Push up with your arms, hands flat on the deck. Arch your back as the wave picks up the back of the board to keep the nose from pearling.

involved is half the battle – if you know what you're supposed to be doing before you start, it will make the whole thing come naturally much more quickly.

At first you'll probably find it difficult, if not impossible, to get from lying down to standing up in one quick, smooth movement. Don't worry about this. You may find it easier to learn the whole thing in stages – prone, kneeling, crouching then standing. If this is easier for you, go for it. However, try to avoid getting into the habit of kneeling as it's more difficult to get to your feet quickly from a kneeling position. Good style, in the long run, is about a quick and fluid movement from lying to standing. Stick at it, you'll get there eventually!

3. Slide your legs up so your leading leg/foot is just beneath your chin, and your rear foot about shoulders' width behind. Your front foot should be at a slight angle to the centre line of the board, the rear foot between 45 and 90 degrees to it.

4. By shifting your weight between your front and back foot you'll be able to lift up the nose of the board or push it down, which slows it down or speeds it up respectively. From here let the board take you in a straight line toward the beach.

Wipeout! Note how Flynn covers his head for protection as he bails. This isn't always possible in an unexpected or high-speed wipeout, but try to remember to protect your head with your arms and hands when you're surfacing.

# *WIPEOUT!*

No one said this was going to be easy, and one thing you'll do a lot is wipeout – guaranteed. But even this has a 'technique' to it. When you feel you're losing your balance, try to fall away from the board and land in the water as flat as you can. This lessens the chances of you being hit by the board, and of bouncing off the bottom – hard-packed sand can feel as solid as concrete if you hit it with too much force. In most cases you'll know you're about to wipeout before it happens – it's pretty rare to have a totally unexpected wipeout.

In small waves wiping-out can be a laugh – in bigger waves it can be serious. Even in small waves though, especially when you're learning and probably nose-diving, the board may be flung into the air after you take a pearler and can easily land on top of you. Always cover your head with your hands and arms for protection, and try not to surface immediately – count to three first, so the board has time to land.

In bigger surf you should try to fall away from the impact zone (the area where the wave is breaking) as well as away from the board to ensure you don't get churned around and held under too long. Try to go into a ball and roll with the wave, especially if you're surfing a reef break (not that you should be at this stage) as it will lessen the chances of hitting the bottom. If you get held under, don't panic! (Easier said than done.) If at all possible, suck in a good lung full of air before you hit the water, and open your eyes once under so you can swim to the surface avoiding turbulent patches of water. Once you're on the surface, check straight away to see whether another wave is about to break on you – at least you can be prepared for another hold-down.

When you surface after a wipeout, remember that your board is attached to you by a leash, which can occasionally act like a rubber band and bring the board winging back across the water towards your body. You'll soon get some idea of whether this is likely from the amount of pull on your leg. If the board is pulling hard on the leash it probably means it is at full stretch and may come back quite quickly once the pressure eases.

Whatever the situation, it's always best to surface with your hands and arms shielding your head to ensure that you don't end up with a fin through the skull. Above all, try not to panic. Most waves will rarely hold you under for more than four or five seconds.

## BOARD RECOVERY AFTER A WIPEOUT

If you wipeout in water that is too deep to stand in, you need to scramble back onto your board without the assistance of a 'foot-up'. To do this get yourself midway along one side of the board, grab each rail, and submerge the back end of the board so you can 'float' onto it. Then simply adjust your position – you may have to slide forward a bit – and paddle back out.

**Even the best fall off. Flynn Novak demonstrates one of the universal truths of surfing – everybody wipes out sometime.**

# *LEFT, RIGHT, LEFT*

Once you feel confident about riding the board in a straight line towards the beach you can start learning basic manoeuvres. To be honest, turning a surfboard in white water doesn't have a lot in common with pulling turns on an unbroken wave, but the main aim at this stage is to become more confident standing on the board, and to develop a better feel for what this length of fibreglass is capable of doing under your command.

So, once you've caught a broken wave and are on your feet heading towards the beach, have a go at turning left or right. The board will only turn to a limited degree, as the white water on either side will tend to push it back shorewards, so try the turns when you have as much speed as possible – that means as soon as you get to your feet, when the momentum of the board will act against the white water.

Turning a surfboard is all about weight placement, and most of the weight is invariably placed on your rear foot/leg. Assuming you're a 'natural' surfer – you surf with your left foot forward – and you want to turn right on the wave, you should put your weight on your right (or rear) leg whilst leaning and twisting your upper body right, arching your back slightly and holding your arms out to your side to aid balance. If you want to turn left, again put your weight on your back foot, but this time weight your upper body to the left and very slightly backwards. For goofy-footers (like Flynn here) who surf with the right foot forward the process is simply reversed.

Turning the board so that you face the wave as you're riding is surfing 'forehand'. Turning so that you have your back to the wave is surfing 'backhand'. Most surfers – even experienced ones – find it easier to surf forehand, so don't worry if you feel a little uncomfortable on your backhand.

# *ANGLED TAKE-OFFS*

Angled take-offs allow you to start traversing the wave immediately you get to your feet. As a beginner this avoids the difficulty of pulling off a bottom turn. For more experienced surfers it allows them to beat sections of breaking or broken water, or to stay ahead of the lip of a fast-breaking wave and maybe even let them get barreled. On a broken wave, have the board angled very slightly left or right as you take off – not too great an angle though, or the wave will probably lift the side of the board and push you off.

The more quickly you can get to your feet the more effective an angled take-off is in traversing the wave, and the fact that you've taken off at an angle should enable you to ride the wave diagonally towards the beach.

**Taking-off at an angle sets you up in the right direction to ride across the wave.**

# HELPFUL HINTS

Learning to get to your feet is the hardest part of learning to surf, and can be the most demoralising if you're making slow progress. You can help yourself by:

1. Getting as fit as possible before you start learning.
2. Persevering – if it doesn't come straight away, don't give up! We all have different learning abilities and rates of uptake. Just because you may be slower than your friends at getting to your feet initially doesn't mean that you won't be as good or even better once you have actually learnt to stand up – seriously!
3. Being motivated. If you really WANT to learn to surf, you'll undoubtedly achieve your aim.

# COMMON MISTAKES

The old saying 'you learn from your mistakes' is very true. Here are the most common ones amongst beginners. If you know what they are you'll know how to avoid them. Maybe!

1. Kneeling before standing up.
2. Weight too far forward on the board, which can lead to pearling, or weight too far back which can make it difficult to catch waves.
3. Getting to your feet in stages – it should be one quick, fluid movement.
4. Trying to stand up before the wave has been caught properly.
5. Too stiff and upright once on your feet – bend ze knees and maintain flexibility.
6. Feet too close together.
7. Feet/body not at correct angle.
8. Not shifting body weight to vary speed and/or turn the board.

## SURF TIPS

- Don't push the board ahead of you when wading out – a wave could easily push it back into you.
- If you surf with your left foot forward you're a 'natural' foot surfer. Right foot forward and you're a 'goofy'. This is ancient surf terminology – don't let anyone tell you they're taken from snowboarding or skating!
- Watch where you're landing when you wipeout and try to avoid hitting anyone else with your board.
- After a wipeout always surface with your hands and arms protecting your head.
- The golden rule of wipeouts, especially bad ones, is try not to panic. It's very rare to be held under for longer than you can hold your breath – unless you're out in bigger waves.

The largest breaking wave ever recorded was around 112 feet/34 metres high.

# Into the Surf

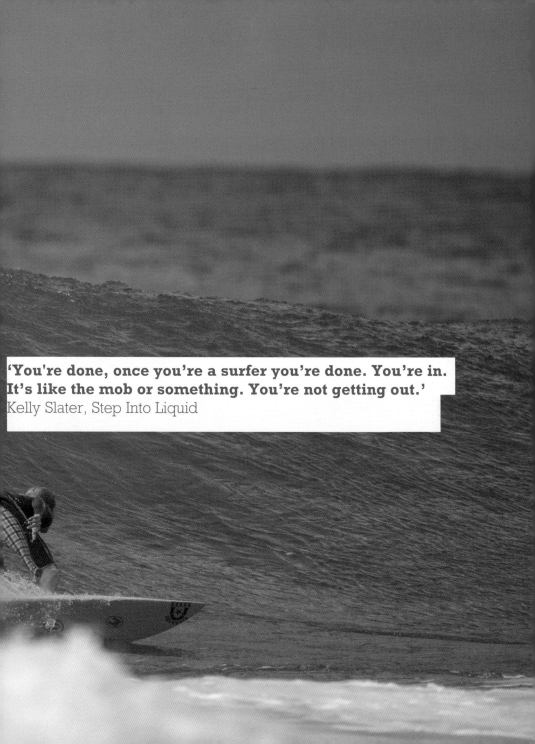

'You're done, once you're a surfer you're done. You're in. It's like the mob or something. You're not getting out.'
Kelly Slater, Step Into Liquid

**'I could not help concluding this man had the most supreme pleasure while he was driven so fast and so smoothly by the sea.'**
James Cook

Once you've got the hang of riding the white water straight into the beach you'll be wanting to get out where the real waves are. But you don't want to be looking for anything very big just yet, and a wave with a three-foot face is quite adequate at this stage (see 'Wave Size').

In order to ride unbroken waves you're going to have to paddle out through the surf. This will mean fighting your way through lines of white water, learning to paddle efficiently, and learning how to sit on your board – no more pushing off from the sandy bottom now!

Paddling out in nice easy relaxed style, well positio ed on the board.

## *PADDLING OUT*

This is the most strenuous part of surfing. Anything you can do to build up your arms, shoulders and back and make them more supple will be well rewarded at this stage, but you can still be pretty sure you're going to be as stiff as your new board after your first few sessions – stick with it, you'll soon tone up.

If you get a flat day while you're on the coast, why not just go out and paddle your board? It's good exercise for when the next swell arrives, and you even get to see the beach from a different angle – but don't go too far out unless you are a competent swimmer and are sure of local rips and currents (see Chapter 6 for more details).

Having pushed your board out until the water is about waist deep, you should be ready to lie on it and start paddling. Walking out any deeper is just hard work, and paddling is quicker and more efficient. Make sure you're in the right position on the board first. You should have a feel for the board by now, and it should be fairly obvious if you haven't got it right – too far back and the nose will be high out of the water and the board will paddle slowly due to drag, too far forward and the nose will dive making the board difficult to paddle. If you're still not sure you're doing it right, compare the way your board is lying in the water with other surfers around you.

Once paddling you should use smooth, alternate strokes of the arms, like doing the crawl. Keep your hands slightly 'cupped', with each hand and forearm entering the water smoothly and sweeping low across the water surface before doing so. Too high is wasting your energy; too much splashing is a sign of poor style. Try to apply equal paddling force with each stroke – if one arm strokes more powerfully than the other you'll find yourself heading out to sea at an angle, although this is obviously the way to turn the board when you need to do so.

At the same time as you're paddling you should have your back arched and your head raised so you can see what's happening in front of you – particularly useful if a big set comes through! Don't arch your back too much as it'll cause excessive strain, especially on the lower back.

# WAVE SIZE

### 'Those surfers who measure from the back have already missed the wave.'
Quote from old Hawaiian surfer to legendary surfer and oceanographer Ricky Grigg

Estimating wave size is a vague science at best – a 3-foot wave in Hawaii, for example would be rated by less experienced surfers at 6-feet or more in somewhere like the UK and Europe. This is because it's the swell that's being measured in Hawaii rather than the wave that is the product of that swell hitting the coast, and wave faces are invariably considerably larger than the swell that produces them since the actual face of the breaking wave will rise up and peak before breaking, an easily observed phenomenon at any break.

Elsewhere there's often a 'macho' element to the sport that underestimates wave size – it's supposedly cool to call a wave that is quite obviously overhead '3 to 4 feet'.

So for the purposes of this book we'll assume that like most people you're checking out the wave face as seen from the beach (as opposed to the swell as measured out in open ocean) so that a three foot wave will be around waist high on the average adult, and a 6-footer about head high.

If you're worried about describing wave sizes to fellow surfers, just use terms such as 'head high', 'double overhead', etc. – no-one can argue with that.

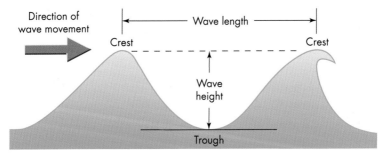

**Physical characteristics of a breaking wave.**

# WARMING UP

It also makes good sense to do a warm-up routine before entering the water, stretching the arms, neck, shoulders, upper and lower back in particular. Find a sequence of exercises that allows you to do this on the beach before you paddle out – ok, it may look a bit pretentious, but if it's good enough for the pros (check them out stretching before their heat in a contest) it's got to be good enough for you.

The reason for stretching is quite simple. Loosen up the muscles that will be doing most work and they're less likely to become strained or injured when you give them some serious stick out in the surf. If you strain a muscle out on the water it will be uncomfortable at best and agonizing at worst, and it could put you out of the water for days if not weeks, particularly if it's in your back. It's also not much fun trying to get back to shore with a bad back.

What we've covered so far in terms of paddling assumes you've been practising in flat water, which is actually the last thing you want if you're learning to surf. In the real world you'll initially be paddling out through small waves, but even then you can sometimes get 'caught inside' by a bigger set or a 'sneaker' wave (a wave that is bigger than everything else that has been coming through). This ought to be a bit of a worry when you consider that research indicates that one wave in a thousand (maybe one every 4 hours) can be twice the average size. From my own experience, though, I'd say it's less frequent than this, but there are occasions when a 3-foot break will suddenly be invaded by a rogue 6 footer. This is why bigger surf isn't the best place to learn to surf – imagine being out in 5-foot surf when that one in a thousand wave arrives!

# GETTING THROUGH A BROKEN WAVE

## DISCARDING THE BOARD

As a beginner, your first instinct when caught inside will probably be to ditch your board and dive deep to avoid being pummelled by white water. That is fine at the early stages as long as there's no-one behind you!

If you're going to discard your board always check first that you're not putting anyone else at risk – if there's a chance your board may hit someone, do all you can to keep hold of it.

Assuming it is safe to ditch your board, you can either dive head first beneath the oncoming wave, or slide off the side of your board and, using it as a platform, push up on it, then sink feet first below the wave. This is usually all you need to do in smaller surf. As with a wipeout, don't forget to protect your head from your board when you surface.

# HOLDING ONTO THE BOARD

If you decide to try holding on to your board whilst in water that's deep enough to stand in, slide off the side as the wave approaches, hold the rails tight with both hands, and push the nose underwater just before the wave hits you. The wave may push you back a bit, but you won't lose time retrieving a ditched board.

In smaller waves you can also move forward on the board as a wave approaches, and push the nose under the water just before the white water hits you. Lie flat on the board holding the rails, and let the white water wash over you, then slide back and continue paddling. A couple of hard paddling strokes just before the wave hits will give you a bit more momentum to get through it.

Another option in small waves is simply to push up with your arms and lift your upper body away from the board, so that the white water passes between you and your board. Or, if you're sitting on your board while out in small surf you can 'get through' a breaking wave by turning your back to the white water, remaining sitting and leaning back into the wave while gripping the board with hands and legs; then turn back round to face out to sea once the wave has passed. At this stage you may find this technique a little awkward.

**The surfer lies flat on the board and allows this small wave to roll over him, comfortably making it through the wave.**

Leaning back on the board. The resistance of the surfer's body weight and the board prevent a small wave from pushing him back into the beach.

Surfboards in 1900 were up to 16 feet (5 metres) in length.

**An Eskimo roll. As the wave approaches the surfer rolls the board, clinging hard to it from underneath while the wave passes over head.**

## 'ESKIMO ROLL'

An Eskimo roll requires a reasonably good feel for your board and is not something you'll be able to do straight away. However, with bigger boards such as mini-mals and longboards this may be the only really effective way of getting through larger waves while keeping hold of your board.

You need to hold the rails tight, and roll upside down as the wave approaches, holding tight onto the board. If you keep the board flat in the water the wave should roll over the top of it and leave you more or less where you started from. Remember to keep a tight hold, otherwise the wave can easily rip the board out of your hands. Once the wave has passed over you, flip the board back over, clamber back on, and continue paddling out.

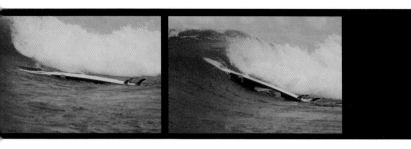

A duck dive as a surfer heads out for unbroken waves. (The photos give the view from the beach, the drawings the underwater perspective.) As the wave approaches, the surfer pushes the front of the board down to duck beneath the wave. As the wave rolls over him he transfers his weight to the back of the board using his knee. This forces the nose up and it pops out of the back of the wave. Done properly, he can continue paddling out with very little loss of momentum.

## DUCK DIVE

This is a technique used by experienced surfers, and you shouldn't feel under any pressure to be performing duck dives at this early stage. However, it's worth knowing about so that when you're more confident in the surf you can start having a go. It's easily the most efficient way of getting out through the surf.

As the wave approaches, push up on your board and use your weight to push the front of the board under the water, either just at the base of a breaking wave, or just in front of a broken wave. Once the front of the board has submerged and the wave is passing over you, push the tail down with one knee. The pressure on the back of the board should be enough to push the nose up, so that as the wave passes you surface through the back of the wave to carry on paddling.

This is not an easy manoeuvre. It needs practice, timing and a cool head, but as soon as you feel confident enough to give it a try, go for it – the sooner you start the sooner you'll get it wired.

A wave approaches the beach at 15–20 miles per hour.
A wave will break in a water depth roughly 1.3 times the height of the wave face.

## SITTING ON THE BOARD

Once you've fought your way out past the white water you'll probably feel like a well-earned rest before you try to catch a wave. Sitting on your board in the line-up is a good way of getting your breath back and checking how the swell and waves are behaving. However, as with paddling, sitting on a board isn't quite as easy as it may seem.

Practice finding a sitting position on the board in which you feel most stable – this will invariably be with the front of the board out of the water and the back end submerged (as you'll see from the other surfers around you). You can turn the board while sitting on it by using your legs as paddles as well as your arms. Remember to help yourself by making sure the deck has a good coating of wax before you hit the surf.

**Sitting on the board – looks nice and easy, doesn't it? But even this requires practice.**

## SURF TIPS

- Paddling out will be hard work at first – expect to have aching upper body muscles!
- Always do warm-up exercises before you go out into the surf – loosen up so you can hang loose!
- Try not to ditch your board when faced by an oncoming wave – holding on to it is safer and more efficient surfing.
- Never paddle out directly behind another surfer – if he/she loses their board after being hit by a wave, guess who it's going to hit?

# Surf Manoeuvres

'You can't stop the waves, but you can learn to surf.'
Jon Kabat-Zinn, scientist and meditation teacher

**'It's a sunny day, waves are peeling off, my surfboard is in the back of my car ... damn, I love it!'**
Chris Isaac, musician and surfer

Once you've become competent at catching and riding broken waves you'll soon want to ride the unbroken face – this is 'real' surfing. A number of basic manoeuvres are described in some detail in this chapter – when you can do all of these you can with some justification call yourself a competent surfer. More advanced manoeuvres are described briefly at the end of the chapter, but since the book is aimed at beginners, I haven't gone into great detail about manoeuvres that you're unlikely to be pulling off until well beyond the beginner and book stage.

Surfing an unbroken wave requires a good feel for your board and a reasonable level of confidence in the surf and half a dozen rides to the beach on white water won't give you either of these attributes. Take time to learn the elementary stages, and you'll benefit far more when you eventually head out the back.

# *THE TAKE-OFF*

This is the point at which the whole ride begins, so you need to get it right – otherwise it could end up being a very short ride! There are two methods of taking off:

A forehand angled take-off. Flynn is already sighting 'down the line' as he gets to his feet, with the board travelling diagonally to the wave face.

Inside out

The inside rail refers to the edge of the board nearest the wave face. The outside rail is the edge furthest from the wave face – and usually nearest the shore.

# ANGLED TAKE-OFF

As the name implies, this involves taking off at an angle to the wave. It saves having to do a bottom turn (see below) which makes it easier for many beginners.

As the wave approaches, paddle at a slight angle to the shore and the face of the wave. As the wave picks up the board, you will find it's already starting to progress along the face of the wave. At this stage you should try and get to your feet. This will be more tricky than on the broken waves you were surfing previously. You need to do it more quickly so the white water of the broken wave does not have time to catch up with you, and you also need to have better balance to compensate for the fact that the board is moving at an angle rather than straight forward. Once on your feet adopt a slightly crouching stance with arms apart for balance, and sight along the face of the wave. You'll need to shift your weight from foot to foot to get the board 'into trim' – this basically means getting it onto the fastest, most powerful part of the wave.

This description assumes you've gone for a forehand take-off. Most surfers favour riding waves forehand as it's generally regarded as easier, mainly because you can see the wave face and what the wave is doing close to the curl. That said, some beginners seem to find backhand waves easier to start with – I did, for one. If you're going for a backhand angled take-off, it's pretty much the same as doing it forehand although you need to take off at an angle which is a little tighter to the wave. Trimming is more difficult as you cannot see the wave so readily on your backhand, and there can be a tendency to stall the board and lose speed. But don't let this put you off surfing on your backhand – if you only ever surf forehand you're gonna severely restrict the number of breaks you can ride!

**A backhand angled take-off. This take-off has allowed Flynn to just stay ahead of the white water and head down the line at speed.**

A forehand bottom turn. Flynn pushes down hard on the inside rail and goes into a perfect bottom turn. Note the way his 'body' stores the energy of the drop down the face; the front foot 'guides' the board round; and he constantly looks ahead to where he intends to go next.

A backhand bottom turn. Flynn has dropped down the face of the wave, body poised for the release of energy at the bottom ready to turn the board back up the face. Note the use of the arms for balance at the point of turning.

# THE BOTTOM-TURN

## FOREHAND BOTTOM TURN

Paddle for the wave. As it picks you up, get to your feet as quickly as you can, then ride the board straight down the face of the wave. At the bottom of the wave push down with your feet and body weight onto the inside rail, with more pressure on your back foot so the tail and fins are also cutting into the wave at the same time as the inside rail. Guide the board round until you're either heading back up to the lip or have straightened out ready to trim along the face. Your body should move smoothly so that at the bottom of the wave your legs are bent, storing energy like a spring that is then released smoothly but quickly to direct the board along the arc of the turn. If you try to 'throw' your body and board into the turn you'll more than likely fall off.

# BACKHAND BOTTOM TURN

This is more difficult than a forehand turn. Many people also find it harder to lean into a turn on their backhand than their forehand. Despite this, the manoeuvre is essentially the same as a forehand bottom turn. Take off straight down the wave, bend your knees and lean into the turn with your weight on the tail and inside rail and guide the board round ready for your next move. You should have your feet almost parallel for this move, and your body weight needs to be angled back towards the face of the wave.

**Flynn pulls off an absolutely classic cutback at Pipeline.**

Two things to remember. If you put too much weight on your inside rail and/or tail the board may stall, making it difficult to regain enough speed to stay on the clean face of the wave – or you may even wipe out. If you put too little weight on the inside rail and/or tail the board won't respond enough to get you round the arc of your turn before the lip lands on top of you.

# THE CUTBACK

Once you've mastered these manoeuvres you'll eventually need to learn how to do a cutback. This is used to get you back towards the pocket of the wave, where the power centre is, from out on the face where power is diminished. It's a tricky manoeuvre that involves the essentials of forehand and backhand turns and until you have these mastered you'll have problems with effective cutbacks.

## FOREHAND CUTBACK

Although a cutback is an excellent way to get back to the most powerful part of the wave, timing and positioning are highly important when going for it. If you cutback too soon you may get caught by the white water of the breaking wave; if you do it from too far out on the face you may not have enough speed and power to get the board all the way round, resulting in a stall.

Once you're out on the face of the wave, take the board as high up the face as you can before transferring your weight to the outside rail. Twist your head and upper body round towards the direction in which you aim to go, which is back towards the curl, then put your weight on to your back foot and guide the board round so you are now riding backhand towards the approaching white water. Use your arms for balance throughout the manoeuvre.

Before you hit the white water, start to angle the board around and back in the direction you've just come from. This means once again putting weight on the outside rail and the tail, and weighting your upper body much as if you were doing a forehand bottom turn. Use your back foot to pivot on, turning the tail under this pivot. If you get it right the board will turn as it becomes immersed in white water (or just before), and you'll find yourself back in the most powerful part of the wave.

For something that's supposed to be a 'basic' manoeuvre, a cutback isn't especially easy. This is because it's a relatively drawn-out manoeuvre combining two distinct moves performed so that they essentially flow one into the other. As a beginner you'll probably find it difficult enough performing one manoeuvre at a time, without going for two together. Practise initially by trying gentle turns, and accept that you may get bogged down in white water or stall way out on the face. With practice you'll get there eventually and once you get your cutbacks wired you can make much more of a wave.

# BACKHAND CUTBACK

In some ways this is easier than a forehand cutback, as once you turn back towards the white water you can see the wave easily – on a forehand cutback it's more difficult to see what the wave is doing after your first turn. Once again, get as high up the wave as you can. Then place your weight towards the outside rail and tail, pivoting round on the tail so the board arcs around to face the breaking wave. Now you can see the face of the wave – try to keep your head up – there can be a tendency to look down towards the bottom of the wave as you turn the board.

As you approach the white water your weight will be on the inside rail again (this was the outside rail before you turned, remember?). Gradually transfer your weight onto the outside rail again, although not so gradually that the white water overwhelms you. As the board turns, be careful that the outside rail and the nose don't dig into the water too much – which is a common mistake – before eventually increasing pressure on the tail to swing the board all the way round and set off along the face again. Simple!

**Backhand cutback. Flynn places most of his weight on the back foot and the inside rail cuts sharply into the wave face as he turns the board.**

# THE TOP TURN/OFF THE LIP

On the whole this move is easier than a cutback, with the added advantage that it can be practised at the end of a ride as the wave is closing out – so you have nothing to lose if you wipe out when attempting it. The top turn is a sharp turn performed just under the lip of the wave; the off the lip is a similar turn performed, as the name suggests, off the lip of the wave. There isn't a great deal of difference between the two moves except one is slightly higher up the wave than the other, although a really hard driving off the lip does look far more dynamic. Both moves can naturally follow a bottom turn as your board heads up towards the top of the wave face.

> Large waves can exert a force of more than 3 tons per square foot when they break – ouch!

## FOREHAND TOP TURN/OFF THE LIP

From the bottom turn, guide your board round and up the face of the wave, looking ahead to judge the point at which you want to hit the lip. As you approach the lip, place your weight hard on the back foot so the fins start to cut into the wave face, while using your front foot to guide the board round. Arms are vital for balance here, but don't flail like a windmill!

You need to make sure the board is well into the arc of the turn by the time you get to your highest point on the face, otherwise you may end up too high

Forehand off the lip. Moves like this require an aggressive and confident technique for success.

on the wave and lose it as it passes beneath you. Once the board is heading back down the face you can decide whether to continue all the way down to pull another bottom turn, or to trim along the face. At first, a full-on turn of this type may be more than you can manage. By attempting a scaled-down version, adjusting your weight to move the board up and down the face in elongated 'S' turns, you can approach it gradually.

**A forehand top turn. From a carving bottom turn Flynn heads up the face, placing all his weight on the tail to bring the board around at the lip ready for his next move.**

A backhand off the lip. By using all the energy of the wave to maximum effect Flynn is able to pull off an impressive turn. Note how his weight is transferred from rail to rail, his weight is focused on the back foot and his arms are used for balance.

# BACKHAND TOP TURN/OFF THE LIP

As with most backhand manoeuvres, this is more difficult than the forehand version. Come out of your bottom turn and try to look along the face to the point at which you want to hit the lip. This is harder riding backhand, as you're looking over your shoulder. Push down hard with your back foot, moving weight onto the inside rail so the board heads back up the wave. At the top of the wave, transfer your weight again to the outside rail, and be aggressive with putting your weight on your back foot – make those fins cut in.

It's important to use your arms for balance and shift your upper body to help with the weight transfer. The board should by now be heading back down and/or along the wave. Don't keep your weight on the outside rail for too long, otherwise it may dig in and you'll be thrown off the board and down the face of the wave. From here line up your next move.

# THE KICK-OUT

All good things come to an end, waves included, but what happens when they do? For most beginners riding a clean wall of water, the last thing to worry about is how to get off the wave after all the time and effort they've spent getting on it. However, you'll eventually need to learn how to make a controlled exit – it's safer than just falling off and hoping for the best; it's quicker than falling off as you'll be over the back of the wave rather than under it; and it looks more stylish.

A kick-out is really no more than a top turn without the turn. Simply ride the board up the face of the wave, and as you reach the top stall it by putting your weight on the back so the tail sinks into the face. The front of the board should be just over the top of the wave at this stage. As the board stalls, it will inevitably move towards you because it's sinking under you. As it does so, extend your arms forward, grab the rails, and drop down into a paddling position with the board facing back out to sea. With practice you'll be able to land on the deck in exactly the same position as if you were paddling, and thus move from riding to paddling back out in one smooth movement.

# WHERE NEXT?

The manoeuvres above make up what many people would consider to be the basics of surfing – which is what this book is all about. By the time you can perform all these with confidence you'll be a competent surfer, and this book will have been getting dusty on your bookshelf for some time. So where do you go next? As I said at the start of the chapter, there are no detailed descriptions of advanced surfing manoeuvres here. By the time you're tube riding and performing floaters you won't need a book to tell you how to do it – these moves will be something that come from the experience and skill you've developed from your own ability and determination. However, it's still worth finishing the chapter with a brief description of some more advanced surf techniques so you know what you're seeing out in the surf when you first start surfing, and what you can aim for.

Radical manoeuvres such as those that follow require you to surf in the most powerful and critical part of the wave, so you need the experience to read the wave accurately and quickly. You also need a high level of fitness, and the right attitude – you have to really go for it with these moves, and not worry too much about the consequences of not pulling it off.

# TUBE/BARREL RIDE

The classic surf manoeuvre – a good barrel can live with you forever. Riding inside the lip of a hollow wave whilst surrounded by moving water can look deceptively simple and exceptionally cool when performed well, but your timing and positioning have to be spot on otherwise you've got no chance of pulling it off. Conditions also need to be ideal – a powerful break with a light offshore wind to hold up the face of the wave and allow it to pitch out and barrel.

Weight transfer and trimming is all-important with barrel riding – you need to be able to stall your board by putting your weight on the back foot so that the tubing section of the wave can overtake you, but not so much that you get caught by the foam ball at the back of the barrel which is essentially the broken wave following up the barreling lip. Once the wave is breaking over you it's necessary to adjust the trim of the board constantly, and also to be ready to shift your weight forward to accelerate out of the barrel. It's possible to get barreled riding frontside or backside, but a backside barrel ride is much harder as you can't see what the lip is doing behind you.

Once you've been barrelrd you'll never look back. The addiction will kick in and you'll need to catch another … and another … and another ….

**A tube (or barrel) ride. Flynn constantly adjusts his body weight and the trim of the board to remain covered up.**

# ADVANCED OFF THE LIP

This is an extension of the standard off the lip described above. All but the tail
of the board is brought over the top of the lip, before being brought back
round and down the face.

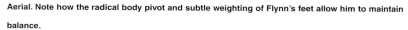

Aerial. Note how the radical body pivot and subtle weighting of Flynn's feet allow him to maintain balance.

## AERIAL

A potential off the lip can be projected into an aerial by keeping the board going up through the lip and out into air as it breaks free from the face of the wave. The surfer usually grabs the rail to keep the board in contact with his/her feet as it travels through the air, ideally describing an arc before coming down onto the face of the wave to continue riding.

# FLOATER

This can be used when a wave 'sections' or breaks in front of you. The board is directed up onto the lip of the breaking wave, then 'floats' across the top of the white water, before eventually coming down with the curtain of water, ideally to continue the ride. It can also be used to finish a ride in which the wave is closing out.

The most popular modern board design, the three-fin 'thruster', was developed in the early '80s by Aussie pro surfer and board shaper Simon Anderson.

Floater. The need for skilful use of balance and weight distribution is obvious, especially as the board falls with the lip.

360. As you can see a 360 is tricky move, not least because the white water has time to catch up with you as you're spinning round, making it difficult to get back onto the clean face of the wave. Check out the cool rooster tail that Flynn throws!

# ADVANCED CUTBACK

This consists of a deeper, carving turn back into the wave, followed by a 'foam bounce' off the white water to get the surfer back onto the clean face of the wave.

**Advanced cutback. Flynn carves the board into the wave face to throw up heaps of spray – his body follows his line of sight then he hits the foam aggressively.**

# 360

As the name suggests, this is a 360-degree turn that is executed high on the face of the wave. It's difficult, because it takes time to get the board round, and it also involves the surfer remaining in one spot on the wave to perform the move while the white water may come past and make it difficult to catch up with the clean face of the wave again.

**Tail slide – skilful distribution of body weight is an essential part of this manoeuvre.**

# TAIL SLIDE

This involves forcing the tail of the board out into a slide along the face of the wave then bringing it back round again to continue surfing along the wave – it takes a lot of strength to push the tail out like this as you're essentially forcing against the direction of travel, and it also needs good skill to bring it back and continue riding the wave.

# MALIBU MOVES

Longboards are ridden 'the same but different' to modern short boards. While good longboarders can pull off most of the moves described above, there are also a few manoeuvres that are generally only practised on longboards. Here are some of them.

> The longest wave regularly ridden is the Severn Bore, England, with rides in excess of 2 miles possible.

# WALKING THE BOARD

In order to get longer boards to trim effectively on the wave, it's often necessary to shift your weight about to such an extent that it can only be done by walking up and down the deck. This should be done in a smooth 'foot over foot' action – never shuffle!

Flynn 'walks' towards the front of the board to improve trim – and it also looks good. Wearing a leash makes this move more difficult as there's always the risk of getting the leash caught around your feet.

# HANG FIVE/HANG TEN

Once you've walked all the way up to the nose of the board, you can style it even further by curling the toes of one or both feet over the nose – 'hang five' and 'hang ten' respectively. A hang ten in particular is an elegant but difficult move.

Flynn, five toes over – balance is everything on this move, even more so on a hang ten.

Surfing dates back at least as far as the 15th century in Hawaii, and probably much further.

## SURF TIPS

- Never forget that you need to shift your weight around on the board constantly, even to ride in a straight line – don't stiffen up.
- Don't thrash around like a headless chicken either – there's no point wiggling your backside around all over the place and waving your arms like a wind turbine if it doesn't achieve anything – and it rarely does.
- Ensure your feet are not too far apart when you stand up. This is a common mistake with beginners, and often results from riding a board that's too short for your ability. This leads to having your foot a long way forward to give the board the necessary momentum to travel along the wave.
- Practice! Go out even when the surf is borderline – the more time you spend in the waves, the more quickly you'll improve.

The first westerner to see surfing was Captain James Cook, when he 'discovered' the Sandwich Islands (now Hawaii) in 1771.

# Safe Surfing

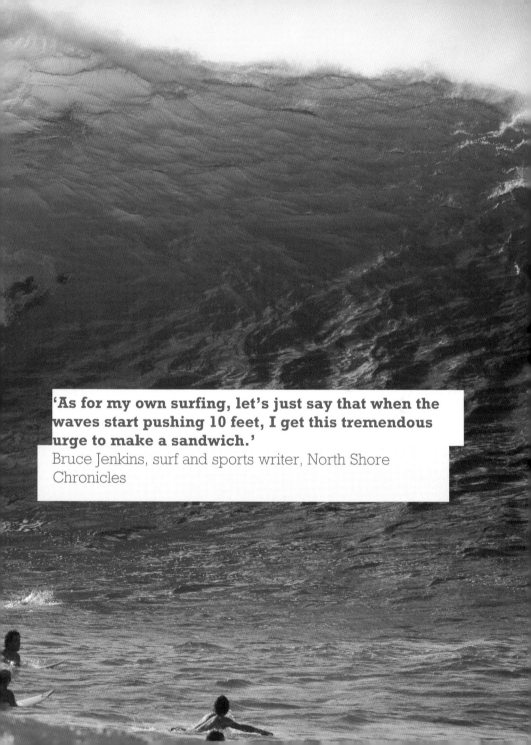

'As for my own surfing, let's just say that when the waves start pushing 10 feet, I get this tremendous urge to make a sandwich.'
Bruce Jenkins, surf and sports writer, North Shore Chronicles

**Once you're out in waves of this size, safety is the major consideration.**

There's no doubt about it – you'll find a level of freedom in surfing that few other apects of life can offer. Even so, you can't just paddle out at a break and do exactly what you want in the water. You need to consider both your own safety and that of other surfers and water-users when you're riding the waves, so this chapter covers the basic common-sense aspects of surfing that are often overlooked by both beginners and experienced surfers alike.

# ON THE BEACH

**Safe bathing – learn what the lifeguard beach flags mean for your own safety and that of others. A red and yellow flag indicates a bathing area, a black and white flag is for a surfing area.**

**'Every now and then, we would hear reports through the grapevine of big-wave riders on the North Shore [of Oahu] drowning, and for the first time I began to understand why so many of the great California surfers never gave the North Shore a try, or if they did, they came back home and never tried it again.'**
Mike Doyle, legendary waterman and surf champion, Morning Glass

On busier surf beaches you'll usually find that the beach and water close to the shore have been 'zoned' and are patrolled by lifeguards. The zoned areas are set aside for various activities, with one or more areas for bathers and surfers. These areas are marked by flags. The generally accepted system throughout the world is that a bathing area will be between flags coloured half red and half yellow, and a surfing area will be between flags with black and white quarters. The surfing area is usually for any form of surf craft, not just surfboards, which can cause problems in itself (which we'll come to later).

An area marked by red flags indicates danger, and neither bathers nor surfers should enter the water. The red flag may actually be flying because a big swell is running and the lifeguards think it unsafe to allow people in the water, but for many surfers these are just the conditions they want! If you choose to ignore the red flags, bear in mind that the lifeguards are under no obligation to assist if you get into difficulties.

In a world brimful of rules and regulations, it may seem too much that even beaches are regulated. However there are sound reasons for zoning. The potential dangers of allowing surfers to ride straight through areas where people are swimming and paddling are obvious – even the most experienced surfer makes mistakes, and in a stretch of sea packed with swimmers the risk of someone getting seriously hurt is plain.

If you're surfing on a beach patrolled by lifeguards, respect their directions, and if in doubt about the surf conditions, hazards, etc., ask their advice – after all, they know their beach as well as anyone.

# RIPS, CURRENTS, TIDES

## RIPS

Rips are channels of water flowing out to sea. They occur where water
pushed up a beach on a swell drains away and back out to sea – I
discovered their power early on in my surfing career when I spent what
seemed like the best part of an afternoon trying fruitlessly to paddle against a
powerful rip off the coast of SW France – eventually a large wave assisted me
to the shore in less than stylish fashion.

It follows that the bigger the swell, the more water is pushed up the beach
and the bigger/stronger the rip will be. Rips form either side of the sandbanks
on which waves break, at river mouths and along headlands. The water is

This rip is easy to see from the air, but not quite so obvious from the beach. You can usually expect
to find water flowing back out to sea in a rip on either side of sandbanks, at river mouths and along
headlands.

deeper in a rip and it's less likely that waves will break here – indeed, rips can easily be identified by their lack of waves and by the obvious channel of rippled water flowing out to sea. The rip will eventually weaken and die as it moves into deeper water.

Experienced surfers often take advantage of rips to get out to the surf more quickly, using the flow of water for a free ride. Beginners should treat them with caution though, as once you are in a rip you can easily find yourself drifting out to sea very quickly. If this happens, don't panic! All you need to do is paddle at 90 degrees to the rip and eventually you'll work your way out of the channel of seaward flowing water. You may now be faced with large walls of white water, however, as you are back in the break zone. This white water will eventually push you back into the beach, but you could end up with a good drubbing first.

Never try paddling against a rip – unless you're the proverbial Son of King Neptune you won't beat it. If you get into serious difficulties off a patrolled beach, raise your arm in the air to attract the attention of the lifeguard (the internationally recognised call for help). If the beach isn't patrolled, try and attract the attention of other surfers. Inexperienced surfers should never go out alone from unpatrolled beaches.

## CURRENTS

Some beaches may have currents flowing horizontally up or down the beach. These may change direction with the turn of the tide (see next section) and increase in strength as the swell gets bigger. Keep an eye open for this phenomenon. At best it may result in your being taken away from the break and having to walk back up the beach to where you started from; at worst you could be swept onto rocks, or in front of a rocky outcrop with the danger of being washed onto it. To ensure you don't get caught unawares by a cross-shore current, take a fix on a landmark on the beach – a house or lifeguard hut for example – and keep checking regularly to make sure you are not drifting too far either side of it.

## SELF PRESERVATION

- Always be aware of your limitations.
- Never go out in surf that is too big for you.
- Don't stay out too long – once you start feeling tired or cold, catch a wave back in.
- Be aware of the effect of cold water or hot sunshine on your body – both can sap your strength without you necessarily realising what is happening.
- Get local advice on possible hazards.
- Check your equipment regularly.
- Never surf alone, and make sure someone else knows where you are surfing.
- Look out for other surfers and water users.

## TIDES

In some areas, tidal ranges can be very large, and there may be a risk of being cut off from your access to the beach as the tide comes in – watch out for this. It is also possible that rips and currents can change strength and direction at different stages of the tide. Local knowledge obviously helps here, and if you don't have it you should keep a check on what is going on as the tide ebbs and flows to make sure you don't get caught out.

## THE 'DROP-IN' RULE

There are few hard and fast rules in surfing, but this is one of them – and it's the most important! It applies equally to all surfers regardless of skill, age or experience.

**The drop-in rule basically says that on any wave right of way belongs to the surfer nearest the peak or the white water. What this means is that if someone else is already riding the wave, you should not go for it.**

The reasons are pretty obvious. Another surfer taking off on a wave already being ridden risks causing a serious collision. This could injure both surfers or damage their boards, and at the very least will spoil the wave for the surfer with right of way who invariably has to take action to avoid colliding with the idiot who has dropped in.

100

**Drop in. Both surfers have taken off more or less together, but the surfer on the right, who is furthest from the white water, has dropped in and must be shot on returning to the beach.**

Although all surfers should observe the drop-in rule, beginners need to be particularly aware of it. An experienced surfer can usually kick off the wave if he or she inadvertently drops in, but this is rarely so easy for inexperienced surfers. Always look along the wave before you take off to make sure there is no one else riding it or in a position of priority.

Every surfer gets frustrated with this rule at some time or other, because no matter how good you are there are bound to be times when a perfect wave comes through and someone else has priority. C'est la vie, and it will inevitably be worse for beginners, as experienced surfers – especially the locals who know their home break – are constantly able to beat you to the wave. All you can do is grin and bear it, and keep practising so that eventually you become that hot local who is catching all the waves.

# BE AWARE

It will by now be obvious (hopefully) that there are a lot more things to look out for when you go out for a surf than simply waves. This is especially so in crowded conditions, which are becoming increasingly common these days, and are the most likely circumstances in which novice surfers will find themselves. With this in mind, here are a few more tips to help you surf safely.

## GETTING CAUGHT INSIDE

This is when a bigger than average set comes through and breaks in front of you – or on top of you. You can reduce the chances of this by keeping an eye on the horizon. If you see what looks like a bigger than average set heading your way, start paddling out to sea so you get beyond the 'impact zone'. It's not a good idea to paddle frantically. You need to keep some energy in reserve in case you do get caught inside – you can then hold your breath as the wave passes over you. So paddle calmly but quickly, and don't panic!

Of course it's easy to advise you not to panic from the comfort of my own keyboard, but as I know from experience there are few things in life less likely to help you remain cool, calm and collected than an unstoppable monster set bearing down on you. When it's happening, as it surely will, bear in mind that the outcome is very rarely as bad as you'd expect – otherwise I wouldn't be sitting here writing this.

We've already discussed how to get through breaking waves (see Chapter 3), but there are bound to be times when you either can't hold your board, don't want to, or simply lose it. If you plan to ditch your board, make sure no-one else is likely to be hit by it. Just before the white water or the lip hits you, dive as deep as you can, relax, and stay down until you feel the turbulence ease – which will only take a few seconds unless you're out in very big surf. Try to open your eyes – that way you can see the white water of the wave easing as you swim to the surface. Once back on the surface, beware of your board hitting you as it returns on the leash and look around to see if another wave is about to break on you. If it is, repeat the above. If not, climb back on your board and paddle out past the impact zone.

If you get caught inside badly and are taking a bit of a beating, always remember that as long as your board is attached to your leg, you have your own flotation device. If the worst comes to the worst, try to cling to it and let the white water push you back to shore.

Canada has the longest coastline in the world at a massive 56,453 miles – and there's a lot of good, if cold, surf there.

## SURFING IN CROWDS

**Crowded house – however good the waves are it's rarely much fun surfing when it's as crowded as this.**

The surfer riding the wave always has right of way, but this is especially important in crowded conditions. Even if you're paddling out this still applies. Try to paddle to one side of the break, rather than straight through it. This is less likely to cause collisions and is also easier than paddling through breaking or broken waves. If a surfer is riding towards you whilst you're paddling out you are the one who should take action to avoid being hit by him or her rather than the other way round – they already have enough to concentrate on in riding the wave. If this means paddling towards the white water rather than over a clean face, so be it.

If you lose control of your board while riding a wave in crowded conditions, try to grab the board so that it travels a minimum distance and doesn't hit anyone.

## USER-FRIENDLY EQUIPMENT

You can reduce the risk of injury to yourself and others by a few simple measures:

1   Fit a noseguard.
2   Blunt the edges of your fins with sandpaper – it won't noticeably change the performance of your board but it will reduce the chance of laceration if it hits you or anyone else.
3   Check your leash regularly for wear – if it has any nicks or cuts, replace it or it will eventually snap at one of these points. Also ensure that the ankle strap is in good condition, and make sure you fasten it securely every time you go out.

## SURF TIPS

- Always remember the drop-in rule.
- Be aware of the surfing and bathing areas on patrolled beaches.
- Never try paddling against a rip. Always paddle across it, at 90 degrees.
- Never surf alone on an unpatrolled beach.
- When out in the surf, keep a constant check on the waves and what other surfers are doing.
- Remember your board is an excellent flotation device in an emergency.

**Caught inside – these guys are using their boards as much to help them stay afloat as to surf on!**

# Waves and

# Weather

'That's the lemon next to the pie.'
Bear in Big Wednesday

Someone once asked whether I got bored surfing the same waves at my local break all year round: 'Surely it's the same wave every time?' Well, as any surfer could have told him, 'No way mate.' It may look the same to the uninitiated, but every wave is different for a surfer – even those perfect point breaks you see at places like Jeffrey's Bay in South Africa.

But while every wave may be different, it can still be pretty much categorised into one of three types – a beach break, a reef break or a point break. The basic features of these are described later in this chapter. However, before moving on it is worth looking at how and why a wave actually breaks (if you want to know more about this fascinating subject check out the excellent *Surf Science – An Introduction to Waves for Surfing* by surfers Tony Butt, Paul Russell and Rick Gregg).

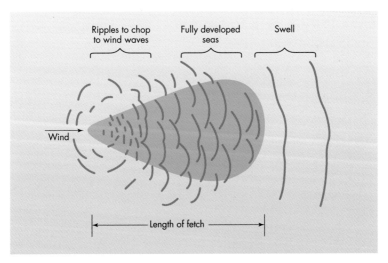

**Idealised development of waves and swell. The fetch (the area of heavier shade) is the area within which the swell is generated by wind action. (From Bascom, 1980)**

# WAVE FORMATION

As everyone knows, the waves that give us our surf are caused by storms out at sea. The further away the storm, and the more intense the associated depression, the cleaner and bigger the waves that appear on the coastline. As a storm develops, the wind blowing across the ocean surface will first of all cause ripples which develop into chop and then wind waves as the wind strength increases. If the wind continues to blow, these wind waves will develop into a 'sea'.

As the waves increase in size, the wind transfers more energy as each wave presents a larger back for the wind to push against. How large the waves become will depend on the strength (force) of the wind, the length of time (duration) for which it blows, and the amount of open water (fetch) over which it blows. It follows that the larger the body of water over which a wind can blow the bigger the waves are likely to be. This is why you can get huge waves in the Pacific, but rarely, in a relatively small sea like the Mediterranean.

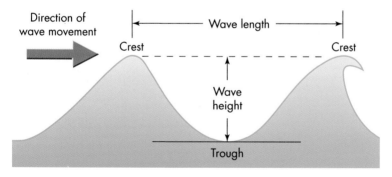

**Physical characteristics of a breaking wave.**

There is a limit to how much energy the wind can transfer to the ocean, and when this limit is reached the sea is said to be 'fully developed'. It will still be a mass of choppy waves tumbling and spilling over each other, and it's not until the waves move away from the windy storm area that clean, even swell lines can develop, radiating downwind from their source. These swells could then travel up to twice around the globe before dissipating, were it not for the fact that other than in the Southern Ocean they invariably collide with land masses, where breaking waves are formed.

As a swell moves towards a coast (usually at speeds of 15–20 mph) it encounters shallower and shallower water until it starts to 'drag' on the sea floor. This increases the steepness of the wave face, making it less stable until eventually it becomes totally unstable and breaks. This will normally happen in a water depth of about 1.3 times the height of the wave, so you could expect to find a wave with a 1-m face breaking in water around 1.3 m deep. This may not always be so, especially in the case of reefs that rise abruptly from the sea floor. The energy released when a wave breaks is phenomenal – large waves have been recorded as exerting a force of 6000 lbs per square foot in the impact zone.

Once a wave breaks, it will take one of three forms:

## SURGING WAVES

These are waves that come in from relatively deep water to steep beaches, and then surge up the beach rather than break onto it. They're of no real use for surfing.

**Pretty bloody useless for anything – a 'surging' wave.**

## SPILLING WAVES

Characteristic of beach breaks, spilling waves are produced by a gently sloping sea bed which causes the wave to peak gradually and thus release energy relatively slowly, so that the crest 'spills' down the face. Spilling waves are ideal for learning.

'Spilling' wave in Hawaii – most other places would be close to calling this a barrel.

## PLUNGING WAVES

Plunging waves occur when a swell comes in out of deep water, and then hits an abrupt rise in the sea bed such as a rock shelf or coral reef. The wave face will steepen quickly as it 'trips' over the reef, and the lip is thrown out to form a hollow cylinder or tube as the energy of the swell is released very quickly. Plunging waves are favoured by more experienced surfers.

There's also occasionally a fourth category, called a collapsing wave – this is somewhere between a plunging and a surging wave and can also provide surfable conditions, although not especially good ones.

**It don't get much more 'plungy' than this – Teahupoo, one of the world's most vicious rideable waves.**

# BREAKS

From a surfer's point of view, waves will generally produce a beach, reef or point 'break', depending on the topography of the coastline.

## BEACH BREAKS

These are the waves that beginners and less experienced surfers should head for, being generally mellower than reef or point breaks. Beach breaks are at their best on a beach where a well-defined sandbar has developed – this will cause the swell to peak on the sandbar, and with luck it should peel to left and right either side of the bar.

**Bliss, bliss, bliss – two people out, sun shining, classic beach break – what more do you want?**

Beach breaks are fickle creatures which will only last as long as their associated bank. This can easily be destroyed by a storm, so you shouldn't assume that a beach that is renowned for quality waves will always have them. For instance, if the banks have been messed up by storm action the wave could become a 'close-out' (it breaks all at once due to the sea floor being a uniform depth beneath the wave), or it may 'section' (it breaks in more than one place along the face at the same time, due to undulating sandbanks).

A good beach will have several beach break peaks along its length that may make it possible to avoid crowded conditions. And since beach break peaks may shift as the swell hits them from slightly different angles, you don't necessarily have to compete with other surfers huddled around the same spot.

As mentioned, beach breaks are ideal for beginners. You should still bear in mind that the beach breaks on a coastline that picks up powerful swells can still pack a solid punch – this means they can drill you into the sand if you wipe out once the surf gets some size to it. Also, as the surf picks up you need to be aware of the development of rips and currents, as mentioned in the previous chapter.

# REEF BREAKS

Reef breaks produce the classic hollow tubing wave that all surfers dream of. These waves are for experienced surfers only, as will become apparent.

A reef break forms where any underwater obstruction rises suddenly above the sea floor – a rock shelf, coral reef, even a submerged wreck. As the swell moves towards the shore from deep water it will come up against the 'reef' which obstructs its forward movement. This will cause the swell to 'jack up' abruptly into a wall of water, throwing the lip of the wave out in front of the face. Under ideal conditions this wall will then peak right or left – or maybe both – to give a fast, heavy wave, usually breaking in relatively shallow water.

The speed and power of the wave is a result of the energy of the wave being dispersed quickly over a small area. This gives a great ride, but can also give a heavy wipeout – and as the wave will be invariably be breaking in relatively shallow water over a hard and maybe sharp bottom, a bad wipeout on a reef break may have serious consequences for both surfer and board. Also, reef breaks generally break in the same spot every time, which means that in crowded conditions competition to get on the peak can be intense. So you need plenty of experience under your belt before you tackle reef breaks.

Classic examples of reef breaks include Pipeline in Hawaii, Brimms Ness in Scotland and, for something hideously heavy, Teahupoo in Tahiti.

**This aerial shot of a reef break gives a good idea of how fast and shallow the wave is.**

Hollow reef break with some lucky dude making the most of the hollow bit.

Lovely Lennox Head in Australia displaying a classic point break set up.

# POINT BREAKS

A good point break will develop where a swell hits a coastal promontory or headland and 'wraps' around this natural projection, often with almost machine-like regularity. As with any swell, waves will form once the swell hits the shallower water inside the headland. This may occur as a result of the deposition of sand from rips and currents running down the headland, and/or from the build-up on the sea floor of rocks and boulders that originated on the headland.

Point breaks provide some of the longest surfable waves, and may run for hundreds of metres down a headland and into a bay. Point breaks can also be quite mellow, and on smaller days sand-bottom point breaks may be OK for inexperienced surfers. However, watch out for the rip that often runs alongside the associated headland. This will get stronger as the swell increases. As with reef breaks, point breaks generally break around the same spot on any particular swell, which can lead to fierce competition to catch a wave.

World-class examples of point breaks include Malibu in California and Ragland in New Zealand.

## SURF TIPS

- Start off surfing beach breaks – they're easier to catch waves on and less painful to wipeout on.
- Learn to read a weather chart for the area where you surf, and work on 'local' knowledge if you want to catch more waves.
- Be sure to check the weather forecast every day, so you know when surf is on the way.

# CATCHING THE WIND

The man in the street is usually of the opinion that good surf requires a howling onshore wind to blow in some 'great rollers'. The surfer in the water knows he couldn't be more mistaken. Ideal surf occurs when a good swell coincides with a gentle offshore breeze, which helps to hold up the face of the wave, makes it more hollow and causes it to 'peel' cleanly.

Internet surf forecasts have negated the need to know how to read a weather chart to some extent, but it's still good knowledge to have, especially as most website reports are based on a generalised computer model that can never compete with local knowledge – the ability to read a weather chart accurately will undoubtedly increase your chances of scoring good waves.

At its most basic, what you should be looking for on a weather chart is a deep depression out in the ocean, while the coastline on which you're surfing is under a nice calm high pressure system.

The depression will be creating a swell that will then emanate from the 'epicentre' and arrive on the coast a day or two later, or maybe more, depending on how far it has to travel – once you get to know local weather patterns well, you can usually predict how long a swell will take to reach your beach to within a few hours. The longer the depression remains offshore the longer the swell will pump through, and as long as the high pressure remains overhead you should get calm conditions, or offshore or maybe cross-shore winds. Then, as the depression approaches land the wind will start to go onshore and mess up the associated swell. If you surf on an indented stretch of coastline or a peninsula you may have breaks that are offshore while others are onshore, so local knowledge can be vital in making the most of a given swell.

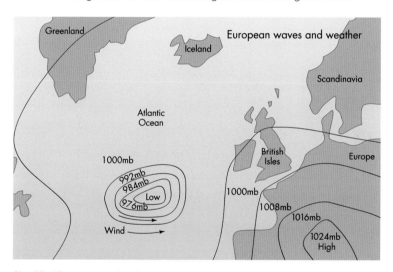

**Simplified European weather chart**

# Surfboard Design

'I'll look at a wave and I can imagine myself on that wave and literally get the feeling in my body, in my muscles of how it's going to be when I ride that wave.'
Kelly Slater, several times world champion

**'... these little boards we have now are really hard to ride'.**
Legendary shaper Dick Brewer tells it like it is!

This chapter looks very, very briefly at the complex subject of surfboard design and basic repairs. If you want to follow the subject in more detail, there are plenty of good books and websites out there covering every aspect of board design and manufacture in great depth. The way a board is actually made is described later in the chapter – to start off we'll look at the different features of a modern surfboard and what their functions are.

## TEMPLATE/PLANSHAPE
This is the basic shape of the board.

## LENGTH
The length of the board from the nose to the tail

## WIDTH
The widest part of the board. On modern shortboards this will usually vary between 19 in/48 cm and 21 in/53 cm, and its location on individual boards will vary from about 8 in/20 cm in front of the centre of the board to about 2 in/5 cm behind.

## NOSE WIDTH
This is the width of the board measured 12 in/30.5 cm from the tip of the nose.

## TAIL WIDTH
This is the width of the board measured 12 in/30.5 cm from the tail.

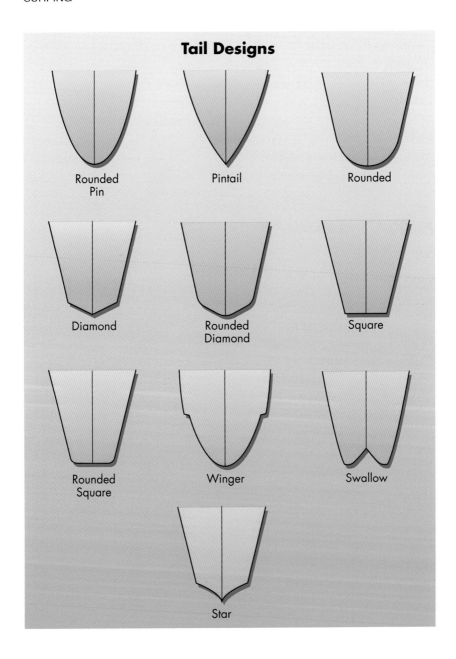

# Tail Designs

Rounded Pin

Pintail

Rounded

Diamond

Rounded Diamond

Square

Rounded Square

Winger

Swallow

Star

# TAIL DESIGN

Tail designs come and go, but those below have all been seen on boards in the last few years, and those that are not so common these days will no doubt surface again in the future.

## ROUNDED PIN

Probably the most common tail shape, and suitable for most types of surfing – it gives smooth turns and holds in well.

## PINTAIL

This is the big wave version of the rounded pin, designed to hold in well in big surf.

## ROUND TAIL

Another variation on the pintail, a rounded tail board is good in smaller surf due to its extra surface area which allows it to pick up the wave more easily.

## DIAMOND TAIL

The sharper corners of the diamond tail result in a sharper turn than from a pintail.

## ROUNDED DIAMOND TAIL

Very similar to a round tail in both appearance and performance.

## SQUARE TAIL

The sharp edges of the square tail result in a very responsive board that turns easily.

## ROUNDED SQUARE TAIL/SQUASH TAIL

Very similar in appearance, both have a similar but somewhat more subdued performance than the square tail.

# WINGERS

Wingers can feature in most board designs, and are usually situated between 3 in/8 cm and 12 in/30 cm from the tail. They combine the ability to hold in on a wave (from the narrow 'tail' behind the winger) with the looseness of a wider tail (in front of the wings). There may be from one to three pairs of wings on a board.

# SWALLOW TAIL

A swallow tail combines the holding-in ability of a pintail (in effect it's two small pintails side-by-side) with the responsiveness of a square tail that results from the extra tail surface area.

# STAR TAIL

A combination of square/diamond tail and pintail, once again allowing the board to hold in well and be responsive in the turn.

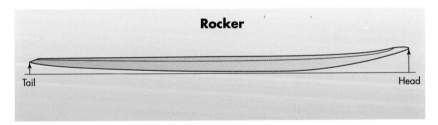

**Rocker**

Tail

Head

**Rocker, nose kick and tail kick play a major part in how the board performs.**

# DESIGN ESSENTIALS

## ROCKER

Rocker is the bottom curve of a board, which is most easily viewed side-on. A very curved rocker results in a board that turns tightly, but is harder to paddle, more difficult to catch waves on and is slower on the wave. Conversely, a flatter rocker gives a board that is more difficult to turn and more likely to pearl, but which will be easier to paddle, will catch waves more easily and is faster on the wave.

## NOSE KICK

This is the upward curve of the bottom of the board in the front third, caused by the rocker. This is important because a lack of nose kick can cause the board to pearl, while too much can lead to its pushing water ahead of it, giving a slow ride.

## TAIL KICK

This is the curve of the rocker at the tail of the board. The more pronounced it is, the tighter the board can turn.

## RAIL

The rail is the edge of the board. Hard rails have a sharper edge and cut through the water more, thus giving a more manoeuvrable board. Soft rails do not cut through the water so readily and give a smoother ride. A tucked-under edge on the rail gives a combination of the qualities of hard and soft rails. Most modern boards will vary in rail hardness/softness along the length of the board.

# Rails

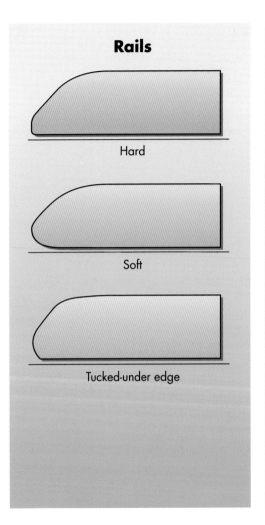

Hard

Soft

Tucked-under edge

# Bottom Contours

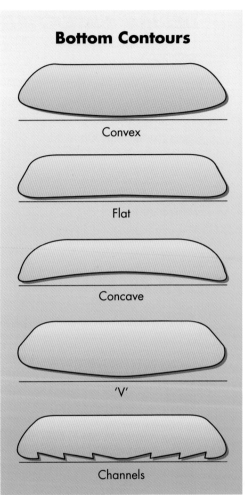

Convex

Flat

Concave

'V'

Channels

# BOTTOM CONTOURS

1.  Convex is the least efficient bottom design – it parts the water like a plough, which prevents the rails from slicing in effectively. However, it can be more effective when combined with other bottom designs.

2.  Flat is a responsive, loose shape, especially in small or 'gutless' waves. However in bigger waves flat bottoms have a tendency to plane a lot, making them prone to 'spinning out' (the tail slides away) in hard turns and more difficult to turn generally.

3.  Concave is good at high speeds, as it contains the water flow down the length of the board and 'squeezes' it out at the tail, increasing the effectiveness of the fins. Its quite common for a board to have a single concave feature at the front of the board, fading to a double concave towards the tail, with a concave either side of the stringer. The double concave splits the water into two channels through the fins and gives a much more maneouvrable board.

4.  'V' bottom boards are often combined with convex bottoms, with the 'V' on the back third and the convex on the front two-thirds. This makes the tail responsive at high speeds, allowing the board to be turned more easily.

5.  Channels direct water flow down the length of the board as they are incorporated at a concave angle. As with a concave bottom, this 'squeezes' water out past the tail, but without compressing it in the way a concave bottom does, as the channels (there are usually between four and eight) run parallel to each other. This allows for easier turning.

# *FINS*

There's been something of a renaissance on fin design in recent years. Until the late '90s most boards came with glassed-in fins, or if they did have removeable fins there would be only one or two shapes to choose from. Now, however, a number of manufacturers produce a wide variety of fins designs for all types of board and relatively few boards have glassed-in fins.

This allows you to alter your fin shape and configuration to suit the type of waves you're surfing, and can make a board much more flexible (not literally!), especially when travelling. It also allows you to remove the fins for travelling, reducing the chance of damage.

Fins arguable have as much effect on how a board performs as do the shape and size of the board, as this brief outline of fin characteristics will show.

# BASIC FIN CHARACTERISTICS

### DEPTH

This is the measurement from the tip of the fin to the base of the board. The longer the fin the better hold it will provide.

### BASE LENGTH

The longer the base length, the more speed and greater the drive a fin will have. Base length is measured at the widest point of the fin, where it meets the bottom of the board.

### FIN PLUGS

The fin plug slots into the fin box on the base of the board and the fin is then fastened in place using a screw.

### RAKE

The rake is essentially the curved area of the fin, and it affects the turning characteristics of the board – the smaller the rake, i.e. the smaller the angle (or offset) between the back of the fin base and the tip of the fin, the better the drive of the fin, but at the same time it will be less manoeuvrable; conversely the larger the rake angle the more manoeuvrable the board.

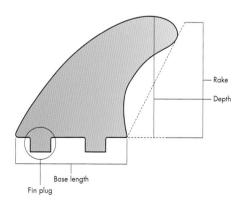

### *FIN FLEX*

This is the amount of side-to-side movement in a fin. Stiffer fins release more quickly in a turn and thus give tighter turns but with less drive; softer fins (and on many beginner boards they'll be so soft you can flex them easily with your fingers) give slower turns but with more drive.

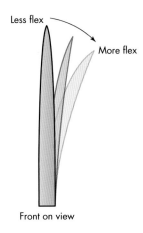

Less flex

More flex

Front on view

## FIN FOIL

Fin foil is the curve of the fin from front to back and tip to base, and this, combined with the variations in fin thickness, determines the amount of flex a fin has when it turns.

Note that a single-fin board, or the centre fin of a thruster set-up, has a foil on both sides of the fin, whilst the outside fins on a thruster have the foil on the outside only and are flat on the inside.

Fin Foil

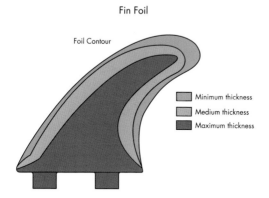

Foil Contour

Minimum thickness
Medium thickness
Maximum thickness

## SURF TIPS

- Listen to the experts and take advice on what kind of board you need – only the very experienced can confidently dictate, for example, how much rocker or which tail shape suits them best.
- If you're buying a custom board, ask if you can see the shaper at work. It will give a valuable insight on how the different board shapes are made.
- Discuss the type of fins best suited to your surfing and the waves you surf with your local surf shop and/or shaper to get the optimum performance from your board.
- Consider having a spare set of fins so that if you do snap or lose one you're not going to be out of the water for any longer than necessary.

# CARE AND REPAIR

Surf gear doesn't come cheap, so it's worth looking after. In particular, custom fibreglass surfboards are very fragile and won't perform to their optimum without care and attention.

At the time of writing, fibreglass boards are still used by the majority of experienced surfers, but they're gradually being supplanted by the recent development of EPS (expanded polystyrene) core surfboards. In essence these are not that different from traditional moulded pop-out boards, except that much research has gone into developing materials such as Surftech's FEPS (fused cell expanded polystyrene) core which is considerably tougher than fibreglass and, the manufacturers claim, waterproof. The great advantage of this is that it's harder to get a ding in the board, and if you do you can carry on surfing and repair it later quite easily with a manufacturer's repair kit (see below). With a traditional fibreglass board, a ding allows the foam core to soak up water and you need to get it out of the water straight away to minimise damage.

Surftech boards cost more than fibreglass boards despite being essentially made from a mould. However, many years of R&D is said to be one reason for the high cost; you're also paying for the durability of the board; and finally, although moulded, the shapes are based on those of world-famous shapers such as Al Merrick, so you'll still be surfing a high performance board.

On the other hand, if you want a board made to your exact specification you'll need to get a traditional fibreglass job, the construction of which is descibed very briefly below.

## CUSTOM CONSTRUCTION

The core of a traditional custom board is a blank made from soft polyurethane foam – as already mentioned this is much, much softer and far more water absorbent than an EPS core. A stringer, which is a thin strip of balsa, runs down the centre of the blank to give strength and rigidity. The blank can easily be worked to the required shape by a shaper, although doing the job well requires years of skill and experience.

Once the blank has been shaped, it may be given a spray job – often as requested by the customer – before the glassing takes place. This involves laminating the blank with fibreglass cloth and resin to give a hard outer surface. At this stage the fins are also fitted. A second coat of filler resin is applied before the board is sanded with an electric sander, followed by a filler coat and finishing with wet-and-dry paper and a polish.

# DING DAMAGE

The glass laminate of a custom board is essentially a lightweight outer skin which has only a relatively low resistance to knocks and is easily penetrated. It could be made more ding-resistant by using more resin, but that would increase the weight of the board considerably; alternatively the board builder could use a material such as carbon fibre, but that would add considerable cost.

If a fibreglass board falls onto a hard surface, collides with another board, or is ridden into rocks, you'll have a ding in your board and a repair on your hands. This needs to be done as soon as possible, or at the very least the hole should be sealed to prevent water getting into the foam. If water is allowed to get in, it will discolour the board and quite possibly delaminate it, lifting the fibreglass outer away from the foam core. If you can't repair your board straight away, use duct tape to cover the ding, or in an emergency board wax can be pushed into a hole to seal it. You must get all the wax out again before you repair the hole.

However well you look after your board it's inevitable that it will collect a ding or two, but there are a few ways of reducing the chances of this:

- Never leave the board standing upright. It can easily fall if caught by the wind or another person.
- Don't wax your board on a hard surface – this can crack the bottom, and any hard projections such as pebbles may hole the board. It also puts strain on the fins.
- Get as good a quality board bag as you can afford.
- When you strap the board to the roof of your car or van, don't overdo it –

you could put a pressure ding in the rails if you tighten the straps too much, especially if they are narrow. (However, do ensure that the board is secure and won't come flying off as you head for the beach.) You should also pad your roof rack with pipe insulation (or suchlike) to give your board a nice soft ride.

**Top surfer Jeff Bushman shaping a new stick for sponsored rider Flynn Novak.**

# DING REPAIR

Small cracks and dents on the board may not always need repairing, but if water is getting into the foam, or you suspect that it is, you need to do an immediate repair job. This is how you go about making a running repair to a small ding:

1.   Ensure there's no water in the ding – leave the board in the sun, ding-side down so it can drain, or use a hair dryer if you're in a rush.

2.   Using a sharp knife, cut out any damaged foam or fibreglass and roughen the area to be bonded with coarse sandpaper.

3.   Small dings can be repaired with resin and catalyst mix (as in the photosequence here), or chopped-up strands of fibreglass or small patches of fibreglass mixed with resin and catalyst. Larger ones will require you to shape a piece of foam to match the hole. Make sure this is a tight fit. Then shape the dinged areas into a slight depression – this ensures the fibreglass that will go on top can lie flush with the board's surface.

4.   If a fibreglass repair is required, cut a strip to match the repair area, but overlapping slightly.

5.   Mix the resin and catalyst. Repair kits will tell you what proportions to use, but the warmer the air temperature, the less catalyst you need. Then brush the resin into the fibreglass over the foam, working it well in.

6.   Build up this area with layers of resin-saturated fibreglass until it's slightly proud of the rest of the board. Alternatively you can pour resin on its own into the depression until it's level or slightly proud of the board – use masking tape to stop the resin draining away (see fig ??? Image 10). Before the resin has set, level out the glass and resin in the depression.

7.   When the resin becomes rubbery, apply a final sanding coat. Once the whole lot has set, sand it down, finishing off with wet-and-dry paper for a smooth finish, and a touch of T-cut for a final polish. Don't get too enthusiastic at the sanding stage or you could go through to the foam.

Major dings can be fixed at home, but they require more experience of board repair, and at first are probably best left to your local surf shop. If you do your own repairs, it's well worth wearing rubber washing-up gloves and a mask, especially in a confined space because some of the materials involved are highly toxic. Always use clean implements. And one final tip – the gunk that's left on your hands at the end of all this (assuming you haven't used gloves) can be shifted with biological washing powder or washing-up liquid mixed with sugar.

For EPS boards, the ding repair procedure is much simpler and quicker. The repair kit consists of a tube of epoxy, which is squeezed into the ding (which should be allowed to dry out first), allowed to set (just a few minutes in warm sun) then sanded smooth.

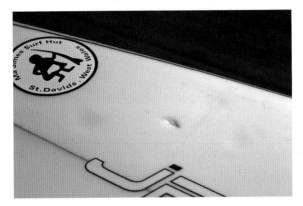

**Time for a repair job! Time and patience plus a clean and clinical approach are needed to get the job done properly, so don't rush – even if the surf is cranking.**

**Clean the damaged area to remove sand, wax, dirt etc.**

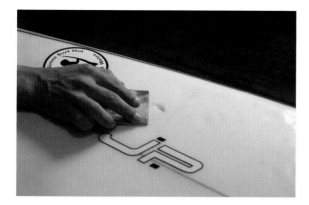

Sand lightly to give the resin and catalyst mix a rough surface on which to bond.

Mix resin and catalyst, following the instructions.

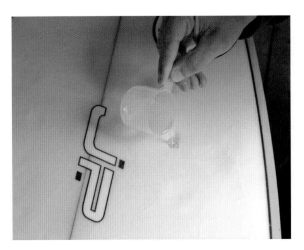

Pour on the mix, leaving it slightly proud as it sets.

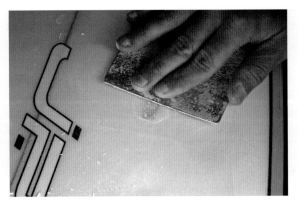

Once the mix has set, sand it down until flush with the board.

**One last rub over with wet and dry and you're good to go.**

# WETSUIT MAINTENANCE

Wetsuits – especially winter steamers – can be a pain to get on and a real pain to take off. It may be tempting to rip off a suit as fast as possible and throw it in a corner until it's needed again, but it won't last long with that kind of treatment. When you consider that for many surfers a wetsuit is the most expensive item of clothing they own, it's surely something that deserves to be looked after.

When putting your suit on, do it gradually, rolling and sliding it over your arms and legs rather than wrenching and tugging, which strains the seams. Fasten the zip carefully too – if it snags, pull it down and clear the obstacle rather than yanking on it until something gives. If you're having real problems with a back zip, ask someone to pull it up for you. If you have a zipperless suit, treat the entry area with respect – they're incredibly flexible but they will rip and tear if you give them too much stick.

When removing your wetsuit, roll it down over your arms, body and legs so that it's inside out. Then ease it over your wrists and ankles.

After use, always try to rinse your 'wettie' out with fresh water. This will help to stop the neoprene from rotting, drying and cracking, and will keep the zip in good order and prevent it jamming with salt. You should also give your suit a very gentle wash in a washing machine once in a while.

If you find tears or split seams, get them repaired as soon as possible – the bigger the damage gets, the harder it will be to repair and the less effective it's likely to be. This may involve sending the suit back to the manufacturer. If the damage is not caused by your own misuse, remember that all good wetsuits should have at least a 12-month guarantee.

You may be able to repair smaller holes yourself using neoprene glue. It's also possible to repair conventional seams using a needle and thread, but if you have a wetsuit with sealed or 'blind stitched' seams, the repair will need a special machine and must be done by an expert or the manufacturer.

## CARE ON SURFARI

Once you decide to travel abroad with your board, you need to pack it properly to make sure it arrives in one piece. Airline baggage handlers may claim to be a much-maligned breed when it comes to respecting other people's property, but with surfboards – well, that reputation had to come from somewhere!

**Surfers have been travelling for decades … on surfari in SW France, 1980.**

When I travel, I wrap every available soft item I can around my board before putting it into the board bag – wetsuit (making sure the zip is not in contact with the board), clothes, towel and anything else. It's also well worth taping bubble wrap around the rails, nose and tail of the board.

All this is no guarantee that your pride and joy will emerge from its bag in the same condition that it went in, so also take a repair kit with you – and get good travel insurance that expressly covers damage to your board.

## SURF TIPS

- Wear a mask when repairing your board unless you're doing it in a very well-ventilated (ideally outdoor) area.
- Treat your board as though it's made of glass and it'll give you much longer service
- Keep a board repair kit to hand and learn to use it – you're bound to need it one day.
- Never rip and pull at your wetsuit to get it on or off.
- Pack your board with real care if you travel by air.

# GREEN SEAS - THE CAMPAIGN CONTINUES

Surfers have organised some pioneering environmental campaigns in recent years through such organisations as Surfers Against Sewage (SAS) in the UK, the Surfrider Federation in the USA, and Surfrider Europe. Here SAS describe their work – and remember that if you surf you have a duty to join one (or all) of these groups.

If you surfed in the '80s or early '90s then you will remember what it was like to paddle out through tampons, sanitary towels, condoms and faeces! The line-up might have been less crowded with surfers back then, but it was packed with billions of pathogenic bacteria and viruses. A group of Cornish surfers who were regularly falling ill after surfing decided to do something about it. As a result, in 1990 SAS was formed to try and clean up the beaches around the St Agnes area. We were soon asked by other recreational water users to extend our scope nationwide as poor water quality affected every coast around the UK.

It's hard to believe it's been that long since the first images of gas-masked surfers appeared in the nation's press marching 'sand-coated booties' off the beach and into London's corridors of power to protest against raw sewage being discharged around the UK's coastline. Maybe that is because we have been lobbying the UK and European parliaments as well as industrial polluters non-stop since 1990. Using a unique and fresh campaigning style but always backed by scientific evidence and real solutions, we set about our task to ensure that the health of those using the water for recreation would be protected by removing the health risks associated with discharging untreated sewage into the sea.

As the organisation moved through the '90s, things began to happen – scientists started working on research that showed there were significant health risks for active water user-groups like surfers, the government started to listen and SAS evidence was used at the highest political level to shape policy.

Undoubtedly this helped lead to a change in approach that subsequently saw water companies begin to adopt better sewage-treatment policies and improve the quality of our bathing water. It's safe to say that your local beach or reefs around the UK will have seen huge benefits from our campaigning.

Unfortunately though, it is not just sewage that provides a threat to our unique coastline and there is still much to do for SAS if our vision of a water environment 'free from pollution' is to be achieved.

Over the years our campaigns have broadened and now and we are working on over twenty campaigns. Issues include:

## CLIMATE CHANGE

Predicted increases in rainfall are expected to overpower our already struggling sewerage system. After heavy or prolonged periods of rainfall we will see more raw sewage and rainwater dumped into watercourses. If we don't tackle this problem we could see water quality slipping back to the murky past of pre-SAS days. But we can all be a part of the solution. Help save energy by lift-sharing to the beach when you can and turning off the standby light on your TV and DVD player after you've watched that surf DVD!

## SAFER SHIPPING

How many more warnings do we need? The UK had the world's first major oil tanker disaster in 1967 with Cornish beaches drowned with oil from the *Torrey Canyon*, Wales has suffered with the *Sea Empress* in 1996, and Scotland and Ireland's coasts are littered with wrecks too numerous to list. We need worldwide action to crack down on the poor shipping practices currently used that continue to allow polluters to go unpunished and owners to use poorly trained crews. We shouldn't have to wait for yet another tanker to douse hundreds of miles of coast with oil, wrecking every surf spot it covers before these crucial decisions are made.

## NO TO TOXICS

With the list of man-made chemical ingredients in household cleaners, cosmetics and paints getting longer and longer and the use of more natural ingredients becoming less and less visible, we started to get concerned. These chemicals often end up going down our drains and into the watercourses. Our concerns proved to be well founded. The Environment Agency (EA) published a study into the effect of endocrine-disrupting chemicals (gender-bender chemicals) on fish in rivers around the UK. This report showed that a third of all male fish surveyed were showing signs of feminisation. We've already teamed up with WWF and helped lobby effectively for the new EU legislation, which will see some of these harmful chemicals phased out. But we need you, as consumers, to flex your Mr Muscles and to choose the lower-impact greener, cleaner, safer alternatives when choosing your washing powder, shampoo, toilet bleach and so on.

## MARINE LITTER

There's hardly a beach in the world that doesn't have litter on it now. We all love to use the beach. To ensure it stays a great place to hang out, make sure you take away all your rubbish! Your local beach might look clean at first glance, but have a closer look and you will often see plastic littered along the high-tide line and above. Plastics can ta e hundreds of years to break down and cause havoc with marine wildlife. For years we have been rolling our sleeves up and doing beach cleans all over the country. We also have the No Butts On The Beach campaign, keeping cigarette butts off the beach as they are made from 12000 plastic fibres and take 15 years to break down. Over the last 5 years we have given out nearly 8000 pocket ashtrays free to smokers. Additionally, we are sending marine litter back to the manufacturers, asking them to reduce their packaging, investigate lower-impact packaging and improving their anti-littering signage in our Return To Offender campaign. You too can do this by downloading a message from the SAS website and popping the marine litter in the post. At the very least after a surf you can pick up one piece of marine litter for every good wave you have just scored.

As we're sure you'll agree, a great deal has been achieved by the organisation since 1990. But sadly for the environment there is a wealth of issues to campaign on, of which we have just scratched the surface in this chapter. To find out more about SAS and all of our campaigns visit the website, give us a ring or pop in. The best way to help SAS tackle polluting governments and industry on your behalf is to become a member! The more members we have, the mightier our influence becomes.

SAS, campaign for clean, safe recreational water for EVERYONE.

www.sas.org.uk
Tel: 01872 553001

# SURF THE WORLD

Surfers have become some of the great explorers of the 21st century, venturing to all corners of the globe where a wave might be found. At one time it was almost exclusively areas of warmer water that were on the itinerary, but with recent advances in wetsuits technology nowhere is out of bounds these days – waves have even been ridden within the Arctic and Antarctic circles.

When you're just starting out you'll probably be happy to surf well-known breaks, which are generally both safer and more user-friendly, but as your skills develop it's only natural to look further afield to more exotic destinations. Here are a few options – none of them could be described as new frontiers, but all will provide world-class waves in the right conditions and, should you find them too busy, you'll invariably find quieter and equally good waves in the vicinity.

# THURSO, NORTHERN SCOTLAND

We start with perhaps the least likely of surf spots, but Thurso and the coastline either side of it gets consistent, quality surf. And it's not as cold as you might expect. Surfers from all over the world travel here to surf the legendary reef break of Thurso East, but beginners can cut their teeth on the nearby beach breaks, or maybe a little further along the coast at the broad, sandy Dunnet Bay.

Experienced surfers may also look to head west along the coast to the heavy reef breaks of Brimms Ness, which has hosted major international surf events in recent years and picks up absolutely any swell going. And if you continue west from Brimms, you'll find some of the wildest, least surfed beaches in Europe.

Facilities are pretty minimal to non-existent so you need to be fairly self-sufficient – bring a good wetsuit (5/3 minimum) and boots, even in summer. Also, don't forget that in mid-summer you get almost 24 hours of daylight this far north so you can literally surf almost all day long.

# *SOUTH WEST FRANCE*

The southwest corner of France has some of the finest beach breaks in Europe and plenty of surf schools, along with summer conditions warm enough to allow you to surf in board shorts and pretty consistent waves.

The stretch of coastline from the Pays Basques area around Biarritz north into Les Landes region as far as the mouth of the River Gironde is essentially one vast strip of sand that on small and medium swells produces waves to suit every standard of surfer, whilst on bigger swells it can be heavy, hollow and challenging.

This is the heart of European surf culture, which means you've got very little chance of finding a wave to yourself – but if you're prepared to get away from hotspots such as Biarritz, Hossegor and Seignosse conditions are rarely too crowded and there are always plenty of facilities for surfers, from surf shops to campsites and bars.

What more could you want? Well, how about fine food and wine, nudist beaches, international surf competitions and the nearby Pyrenees to play in if it goes flat?

# THE CANARY ISLANDS

'Europe's answer to Hawaii' is the tag frequently used to describe Canary Island waves, which means big, heavy and hollow reef breaks – but it's not all like this. Take the massive crescent of black sand that is Famara Beach on Lanzarote, for instance – it has consistent beach breaks that go from almost flat at one end of the beach to head high-plus at the other end on a good swell, allowing beginners to choose the size they feel most comfortable with – and there are also plenty of surf schools to help you master them.

Although all the Canary Islands have surf, Lanzarote and Fuerteventura are the best bets. Fuerteventura is also known for its powerful reef breaks, especially along the island's north shore, but there are also more mellow beach breaks here too, such as Cotillo.

Localism can be a problem, although that usually applies to the more hardcore reef breaks – as a beginner you'll find the islands' 'beachies' are generally quite welcoming as long as you use tact, discretion and avoid dropping in on anyone…

Although described as being within Europe, the Spanish-owned Canaries are actually off the coast of North Africa and are a top winter bolt hole for European surfers, who even in the middle of winter can surf here in minimal neoprene, if not boardies.

# COSTA RICA

A leading contender for the title of 'Surfer's Paradise', Costa Rica's Pacific coast has scores of consistent beach breaks that are frequently ideal for learning on. The water is warm, the waves are usually not too big (although they do have their day) and if you can't get into surfing in a location like this then there there's no hope for you.

Conditions as good as this mean that every man and his dog want a piece of the action, so more popular areas such as Tamarindo Bay, or Guanacaste in the north, are invariably busy with both local and foreign surfers. However, you can find quieter waves if you're prepared to travel – and if you want to have a real surfari, Costa Rica's Caribbean coast has surprisingly powerful waves and the equally good surf of Panama and Nicaragua is within easy reach.

You won't get bored if it goes flat either, with some of the finest national parks in the world, teeming with exotic, Technicolor plants, birds and animals.

# SRI LANKA

Sri Lanka is a surf destination that, once visited, will stay in your mind forever. It's not just the user-friendly azure blue waves that roll onto the island's shores that stick in the memory, but classic palm-fringed beaches, amazing snorkelling amongst reefs alive with brightly coloured fish and sea turtles, thick jungle in which elephants may be seen working, echoes of the British Raj amongst the tea plantations of the interior Hill Country (a good place to escape the heat) and a generally laid back lifestyle that encourages you to forget all about the grind of everyday life back home.

Sri Lanka is the place where many novice surfers step up to riding their first reef breaks, with the focal point of the island's surf scene being Hikkaduwa, to the south of Colombo. It's invariably crowded here, but there are quieter waves all along the coast either side of Hikkaduwa (Sri Lanka's 'Surf City'), and when the surf season on this coast (Dec–Apr) ends, there's the world class right of Arugam Bay to be surfed up in the northeast of the country, with once again alternative waves along the coastline either side.

# GOLD COAST, AUSTRALIA

OK, crowds are inevitable here, but that's a small price to pay for consistent user-friendly, warm water waves in an easily accessible environment. Since surfing is a way of life to (it seems) everyone on the Gold Coast, you'll easily fit in when you turn up toting your board.

However, you'll have to compete hard for the flawless breaks that roll into spots like Duranbah (D-Bah), Burleigh Heads and Kirra. At the same time you'll see a standard of surfing out in the water that is amongst the highest in the world – don't be too fazed if you find yourself sitting beside a world-famous pro or two in the line-up.

If the crowds become too much for you, head south towards the New South Wales coastline where it can be a little less busy.

In between surfing you can do everything from trekking in the outback to diving on the Great Barrier Reef to the north.

# ORANGE COUNTY, SOUTHERN CALIFORNIA

All of California's coast gets quality surf, but Orange County, for visiting surfers at least, is perhaps the most easily assimilated area – it's certainly the California you see in traditional images of the area, with beautiful, silicon-enhanced people strutting the beaches and a hedonistic lifestyle that few other places on earth can compete with.

The waves vary from the ultra-mellow longboard surf of San Onofre in the south to the wall-to-wall fibreglass of Huntington Beach in the north, with the most intense action taking place at Trestles, where perfect waves are frequent and crowds are heavy – amongst them may be some of the world's finest surfers.

If it all gets a bit too much, head south towards San Diego or Mexico, or north to Ventura County where it may not be quite so manic either in or out of the water.

# MEXICO

Mexico's Pacific coastline has heaps of options for travelling surfers – you can have it as hard core as you like in areas such as Central Baja or Oaxaca, or more mellow and user-friendly at somewhere like San Juan de Alima in Michoacan – indeed, this would be a good base for a first-time trip to Central America.

The great thing about Mexico is that whenever you visit you'll find quality waves somewhere along the Pacific coast (although that's a rather glib statement bearing in mind the fact that the coast is almost 4000 km long). This will include everything from mellow beach and point breaks such as those of southern Baja to the super-heavy, hollow beach breaks of infamous Puerto Escondido or the spectacular rivermouth left at Michoacan's La Ticla. And you'll rarely, if ever, need a wetsuit.

The deal with Mexico (as with any other worthwhile surf destination) is do your research first, head for the waves that will suit you (be realistic!), and you're almost guaranteed a once-in-a-lifetime surf trip.

# *HAWAII*

The home of surfing in every sense of the word, but not all the waves are as big and challenging as Pipeline or Jaws – and don't forget there are several islands to choose from. Visit Oahu's North Shore, the location of some of the world's heaviest and most crowded waves, and you'll struggle to get a look in, but try somewhere less frequented such as Maui and there's every chance that even as a relative beginner you'll have a fantastic surf trip.

Here's you'll find mellow beach breaks such as those at Baldwin Beach in Paia Bay, and more challenging but still manageable waves around Palm Point and Lahaina, for instance. And if a big swell comes pounding in head out to Peahi with a pair of binoculars and a picnic and watch some of the world's most daring surfers ride some of the world's biggest waves at mighty Jaws.

# *INDONESIA*

Indonesia has a fantastic array of warm water waves to suit everyone from total beginner to full on charger, and it makes a good destination for groups of mixed ability since the chances are that all of you'll score great waves.

Some breaks, such as the infamous Nias in the northwest of the country, or the much lauded Mentawai Islands off Sumatra, still require commitment and dedication not just to surf them but even to get to them, but ever popular Bali, for instance, is as easy as it gets with good value package deals that can put you right next to easy beach breaks around Kuta or within easy access of the world class Uluwatu, whilst G-Land, arguably one of the best waves in the world, is also easy to get to from Bali.

The down side of the better known and easier accessed waves is crowds, but then that's always a problem when you're starting out – easier waves are always busy waves. But show respect, especially to the locals, and you'll find that something worth travelling for eventually comes your way!

## SURF TIPS

Six travel tips to set you on your way:

- Research – do it. There's no point visiting your chosen destination outside the main surf season.
- Airlines – check 'em out. Some are more user friendly than others – try and travel with one that charges less (or nothing) to take your board.
- Insurance – get it. Both you and your board and gear could suffer on a surf trip so make sure you're covered for theft, health, etc.
- Gear – protect it. Get a good quality bag for your board, and make sure your valuables are stashed safely at all times.
- Health – look after it. Take a basic first aid kit and check on what inoculations are required for your intended destination(s).
- Spares – take them. Repair kit, spare fins, leashes, wax, etc., are all worth considering for more remote destinations – or even just to ensure you can get straight back in the water after, say, a leash breaks.

# APPENDIX: SURFING ASSOCIATIONS

The following selected national governing bodies can advise you about surfing in their respective countries, supplying information that ranges from your nearest surf school to the next competition. For a full list of national governing bodies go to www.isasurf.org, the website for the International Surfing Association.

## AUSTRALIA

Surfing Australia
P.O. Box 1613
Kingscliff, New South Wales 2487
Australia
Website: www.surfingaustralia.com

## CANADA

Canadian Surfing Association
BCSA (on the West Coast) www.BCSA.ca
Website: www.surfns.com

## COSTA RICA

Federación de Surf de Costa Rica
De la Basílica 800 Norte, 125 Este
Frente Condominio Villa Adobe
Santo Domingo, Heredia, Costa Rica
E-mail: info@surfingcr.net
Website: www.surfingcr.com

# FRANCE

Federation Francaise de Surf
Plage Nord - BP 28 - 40
150 Hossegor
France
Website: www.surfingfrance.com

# HAWAII

Hawaii Amateur Surfing Association (HASA)
150 Hamakua Dr. #822
Kailua, HI 96734
United States of America
Website: www.hasasurf.org

# IRELAND

Irish Surfing Association
Easkey House
Easkey
Co. Sligo
Republic of Ireland
E-mail: info@isasurf.ie
Website: www.isasurf.ie

# MEXICO

Federación Mexicana de Surf (FMS)
Calle Sexta #1500
Zona Centro CP 22830
Ensenada, Baja California
Mexico
E-mail: presidencia@surfer.com.mx
Website: www.surfer.com.mx

## NEW ZEALAND

Surfing New Zealand Inc.

9 Bow Street

Raglan

New Zealand

Website: www.surfingnz.co.nz

## PORTUGAL

Federação Portuguesa de Surf

Complexo Desportivo de Ouressa

Av. Almirante Gago Coutinho

2725-320 Mem Martins/Sintra

Portugal

E-mail: fps@surfingportugal.com

Website: www.surfingportugal.com

## SOUTH AFRICA

Surfing South Africa

Robin De Kock, General Manager

P.O. Box 127

Rondebosch 7701

South Africa

E-mail: surfingsouthafrica@gmail.com

Website: www.surfingsouthafrica.co.za

## SPAIN

Federeración Española de Surf
Calle Dolores, 51-53
Entresuelo I
15402, Ferrol (A Coruña)
Spain
E-mail: contacto@fesurf.net
Website: www.fesurf.net

## UNITED KINGDOM

British Surfing Association
International Surfing Centre
Fistral Beach, Newquay
Cornwall TR7 1PH
United Kingdom
E-mail: info@britsurf.co.uk
Website: www.britsurf.co.uk
Website 2: www.nationalsurfingcentre.com

## UNITED STATES OF AMERICA

Surfing America
33157-B Camino Capistrano
San Juan Capistrano, CA 92675
USA
Website: www.surfingamerica.org

# SURFSPEAK

Here's how to make sure you say the right thing out in the line-up.

**aerial:** an advanced manoeuvre that involves taking off from the lip of the wave,
travelling some distance through the air, then (in theory) landing back on the face
of the wave and continuing the ride.

Aerial – self explanatory really.

**ASP:** Association of Surfing Professionals – responsible for organising the annual world
professional surfing circuit leading to the crowning of the world champion.

**axed:** hit by the lip of the wave, leading to a wipeout.

**backhand:** surfing with your back to the wave.

**bank:** sandbank on which waves break.

**barrel:** see tube

Barrelled in relaxed style – Flynn Novak, Pipeline.

**beach break:** surf breaking on a sandy beach.

**blank:** block of foam from which a custom surfboard is made.

**blown out:** term for choppy surf resulting from onshore winds.

**bombora:** a deep water, offshore reef break.

**bottom turn:** a turn at the bottom of the wave face.

**carving:** powerful, high-energy surfing.

**catalyst:** ingredient used to make resin harden (also known as hardener). Very toxic.

**channel:** deep water gap between sandbanks or reefs, or design feature on underside of a surfboard.

**clean:** glassy, peeling waves and/or good surf conditions.

**clean-up:** a large set that catches everybody 'inside'.

**close-out:** a wave that breaks along its entire length simultaneously – no good for surfing.

**concave:** bottom design on a surfboard.

**cutback:** a turn on the face of the wave that takes you back towards the white water.

**deck:** upper surface of a board.

**delamination:** when the fibreglass 'skin' of a board becomes separated from the foam.

**ding:** a dent or hole in your board – get it fixed!

**drop (to take the drop):** to take off on a breaking wave and ride down the wave face.

**Taking the drop at big Pipeline.**

**drop in:** a) taking off as in taking the drop (see above); b) when one surfer takes off on a wave already being ridden by another surfer nearer the peak – the practice of kooks (see below).

**duck dive:** method of getting through a breaking or broken wave while paddling out.

**Eskimo roll:** another method for getting through a wave, mostly used with mini-mals and longboards.

**face:** the unbroken surface of a wave (also known as the green water).

**forehand:** surfing with your face to the wave.

**floater:** a manoeuvre that involves launching the board off the lip of the wave onto a section of broken or breaking wave in front, unweighting, and free-falling down the face with the breaking white water.

**glassy:** smooth seas resulting from calm wind conditions – provides excellent surf when combined with a swell.

**gnarly:** heavy, difficult waves, usually quite big.

Most people would agree this looks pretty 'gnarly' ... especially for the poor bugger caught inside.

**goofy foot:** a surfer who surfs with his or her right foot forward on the board.

**grommet:** young surfer.

**groundswell:** a clean swell with evenly-spaced lines, usually from a distant storm.

**gun:** a big wave board – long and narrow in shape.

**hang five:** to ride with five toes curled over the nose of the board – more common on longboards.

**hang ten:** to ride with all ten toes over the nose – a stylish and difficult longboard manoeuvre.

**hollow:** a cylindrical wave – common with powerful swells and offshore winds.

**impact zone:** the point at which a swell is breaking most heavily and most frequently.

**indicator:** an offshore deep-water reef or bank. Only a big swell or a big set will break on this, so it acts as a good indicator of something big approaching.

**inside:** shoreward of a breaking wave or set (as in 'caught inside'), or an expression for life in the barrel. The inside rail is the one nearest the wave face.

**kick-out:** to make a controlled exit from a wave by riding up the face and over the top.

**kook:** a dorky surfer – the kind that drops in on you.

Kook - and in this case the least popular dude in the surf too.

**leash:** urethane cord which attaches the board to the surfer by means of a Velcro strap.

**left-hander (left):** a wave that breaks from left to right when viewed from shore.

**lined-up:** term to describe an even, well-developed swell.

**line-up:** the point where you sit, just outside the break, and wait to catch a wave.

**lip:** the crest of a wave, which may 'throw out' to create a barrel.

**Malibu board:** another term for a longboard – usually between 8 ft 6 in/2.60 m and 10 ft 6 in/3.20 m in length. Named after the beach in Southern California.

**maxed out:** a break is said to be 'maxed out' when the swell is so big it will no longer break cleanly, but will close out or 'section'.

**natural or natural foot:** a surfer who surfs with his or her left foot forward.

**nose:** the front of the board.

**nose-riding:** technique used by longboarders who attempt to ride as close to the nose of the board as possible.

**off the lip/lip bash:** manoeuvre whereby the board hits the breaking lip of the wave before continuing along the wave.

**offshore:** when the wind is blowing from the land out to sea and holding up the face of the wave – will usually produce ideal surfing conditions, especially when the wind is reasonably light.

**Strong offshore conditions in Hawaii.**

**onshore:** when the wind is blowing from the sea onto the land – this messes up the wave face and produces poor surfing conditions.

**outside, or out the back:** the area beyond the impact zone.

**over the falls:** to fall down the face of the wave inside the falling lip.

**peak:** the point at which a wave breaks first, from which it ideally peels in one or both directions.

**pearl:** this is when the nose of the board buries itself underwater and the surfer usually shoots over the front. Most common on take-offs.

**peel:** a wave is said to peel when it breaks away evenly and cleanly from the peak.

**pocket:** the steepest and most powerful part of the wave, just ahead and under the breaking lip.

**point break:** a break where the waves are refracted around a headland or point and then peel along the inside of the point.

**pop-out:** a machine-moulded surfboard, ideal for beginners.

**prone-out:** dropping from your feet to your belly to ride the board into the beach.

**pumping:** term used to describe a good, powerful swell.

**pumping the board:** a means of increasing speed across the face of a wave.

**quiver:** a selection of surfboards for differing conditions.

**rail:** the side or edge of a board.

**reef break:** waves breaking over a projection rising from the sea bed – usually a coral reef or rock shelf.

**re-entry:** manoeuvre which involves surfing up into the lip of a breaking wave, then coming back down with it.

Re-entry.

SURFING

**resin:** chemical used in a two-part mixture with catalyst to convert fibreglass into a hard outer skin.

**right-hander (right):** a wave that breaks from right to left when viewed from the shore.

**rip:** a channel of water running out to sea.

**rocker:** the curve in a surfboard when viewed side-on.

**sandbank:** an elevation in the level of the sea floor on a beach, causing waves to break over it.

**set:** a group of waves.

**shore break:** a wave that breaks close in to the beach.

**shoulder:** the unbroken face of a wave ahead of the white water.

**soup:** the white water of a broken wave.

**spin-out:** when the fins of the board break loose from the water surface, leading to a wipeout.

**spring suit:** wetsuit with short arms and short legs. Also known as a 'shortie'.

**stall:** a manoeuvre where the board is slowed, or 'stalled', to allow the lip of the wave to catch up with the rider.

**steamer:** a full wetsuit with long arms and long legs.

**stringer:** the thin piece of wood running down the centre of a custom board.

**sucky:** a hollow, often heavy wave.

**switch-foot:** a surfer who can surf with either foot forward.

**tail:** the rear end of the board, which can have a number of different shapes.

**take-off:** the start of a ride.

**three-sixty:** spinning the board through 360 degrees on the face of the wave.

**thruster:** a three-finned surfboard.

**trimming:** adjusting weight and position on the board so that the board retains maximum speed.

**tube:** the inside of a hollow wave.

**vee:** the convex shape on the bottom of a board.

**windswell:** a weak swell generated by localised winds.

**wipeout:** do you really need to know?!

**Going down ...**